# Class 68s



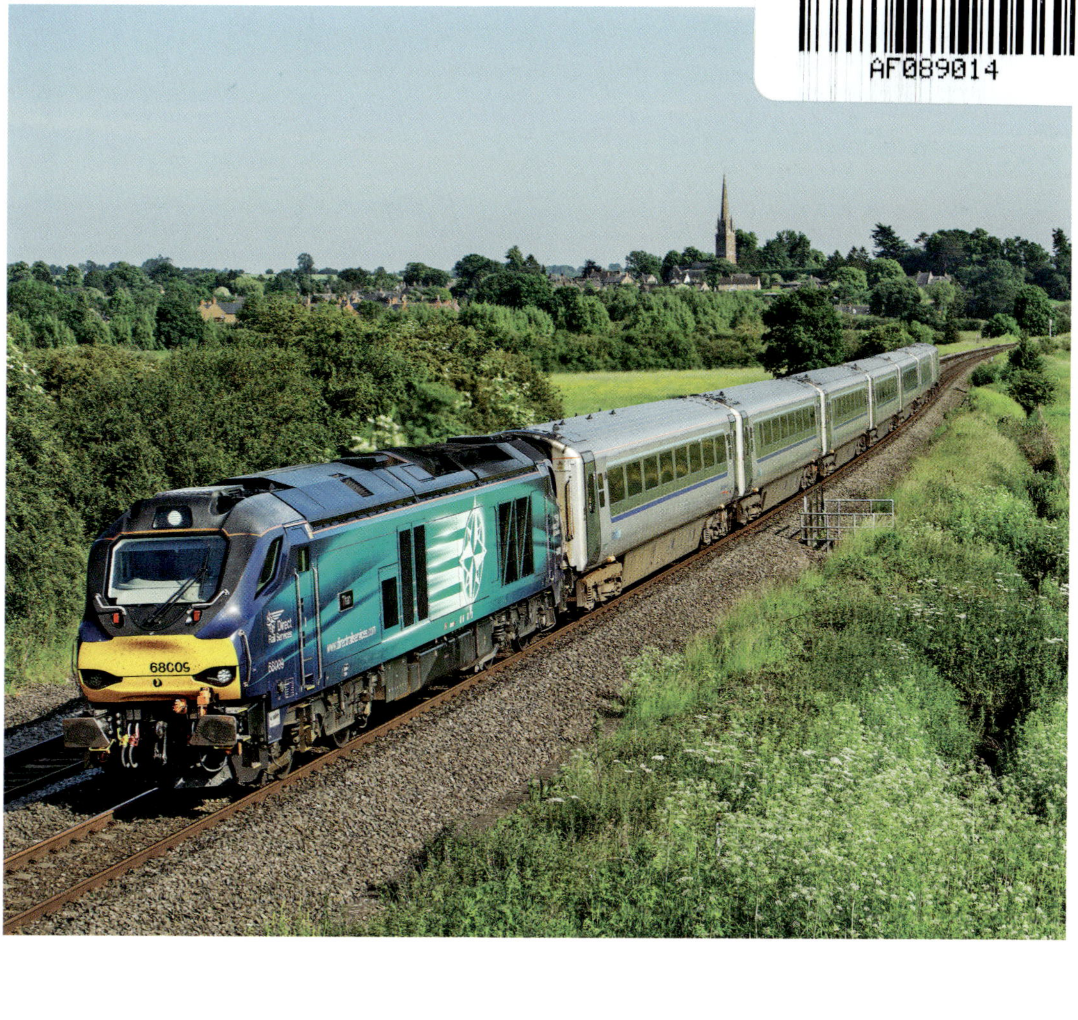

ANDY FLOWERS

KEY Books

BRITAIN'S RAILWAYS SERIES, VOLUME 51

**Front cover image:** With the world famous Sellafield plant on the horizon, 68003 *Astute* passes a row of shacks on the beach near Netherton. Much of the Cumbrian Coast Line passes along the coast with many scenic areas further to the north.

**Title page image:** At the iconic photo location site north of Kings Sutton, with the famous church in the village in the distance, Direct Rail Services (DRS) Chiltern-liveried standby Class 68 68009 *Titan* thunders past while working 1K54, the 18.15 London Marylebone–Kidderminster, on 6 June 2018.

**Contents page image:** With post–Covid passenger numbers buoyant (and with a full and standing train of commuters), 68013 waits for departure at London Marylebone with 1K52, the 17.46 to Kidderminster. In the adjoining Platform 2, to the left, Networker Turbo Class 165 165005 awaits departure with 2A52, the 17.53 to Aylesbury, while to the right, on Platform 4, 165024 awaits departure with 2W51, the 17.24 to High Wycombe.

**Back cover image:** 68028 *Lord President* waits patiently at Cleethorpes, on 19 December 202, in Platform 4. The Cleethorpes (south) route was beset with cancellation issues at the time of writing. Platform 4 is not set up for passenger use and finding a set stabled here means it is in training use only.

Published by Key Books
An imprint of Key Publishing Ltd
PO Box 100
Stamford
Lincs PE9 1XQ

www.keypublishing.com

The right of Andy Flowers to be identified as the author of this book has been asserted in accordance with the Copyright, Designs and Patents Act 1988 Sections 77 and 78.

Copyright © Andy Flowers, 2023

ISBN 978 1 80282 666 1

All rights reserved. Reproduction in whole or in part in any form whatsoever or by any means is strictly prohibited without the prior permission of the Publisher.

Typeset by SJmagic DESIGN SERVICES, India.

# Contents

**Introduction** .................................................................................................................. 4

**Chapter 1**  Technical Specifications ........................................................................ 11

**Chapter 2**  Chiltern Railways .................................................................................. 28

**Chapter 3**  Railtours and Preserved Railway Workings ......................................... 39

**Chapter 4**  East Anglia – The Wherry Lines .......................................................... 41

**Chapter 5**  Cumbrian Coast .................................................................................... 51

**Chapter 6**  Fife Circle .............................................................................................. 59

**Chapter 7**  TransPennine Express .......................................................................... 67

**Chapter 8**  Railtours and Heritage Diesel Galas ..................................................... 83

**Chapter 9**  Special Traffic ....................................................................................... 87

**Chapter 10** Names, Models and the Future ............................................................ 93

# Introduction

With rail freight provider Direct Rail Services (DRS) expanding into locomotive hire, including for the passenger market, in 2009 the company bought a small fleet of locos that was designed to remain in service until at least 2036, and used them to replace much of its remaining heritage diesel fleet, offering in its place a future-proofed mixed traffic loco capable of 160km/h (100mph). This Class 68 locomotive was designed primarily for DRS's main role – transporting nuclear flask traffic. In total, 34 locomotives were built.

DRS approached manufacturers including Bombardier, Brush Traction, General Electric and Siemens with the proposal. Initially, the Class 70 was thought to be a contender for the new loco order (suitably re-geared for 160km/h [100mph]) running and with head-end power added, up to an index of 100 – allowing for the possible emergency haulage of power-hungry stock, such as Virgin's Class 390 Pendolino EMUs.

DRS had originally presumed that the high-power output it specified would mean that a Co-Co wheel arrangement would be needed, though testing with the EuroLight Demonstrator at Velim, Czech Republic, showed that a Bo-Bo design would be able to perform sufficiently in terms of haulage capacity due to advanced wheelslip control electronics.

The small production run that would be needed for a possible one-off design appeared to deter some of the manufacturers. The Rolling Stock Company (ROSCO) Beacon Rail recommended that the manufacturer Vossloh be approached, with the idea that it would be able to adapt its EuroLight loco for UK use relatively easily, and previous work in adapting continental and world loco designs into the Class 67 bodyshell had proved beneficial.

68014, 37402, 9707 British Rail (BR) Mk 2F DBSO, owned by DRS at that point, now with LSL at Crewe) and 68007 *Valiant* inside Carlisle Kingmoor traction maintenance depot (TMD) on various exams and repairs on 14 February 2017. (*Dougie Black*)

On 15 June 2022, 68033 *The Poppy* and 68034 were sent light engine from Manchester to Wolverton for modifications to their AAR (multiple working) systems in connection with their standby passenger duties with TransPennine Express (TPE). They are seen here passing Cathiron, between Nuneaton and Rugby on the West Coast Main Line. Since being released from Wolverton, the two DRS-liveried standby locos have been regular performers with TPE.

The Vossloh/Stadler Class 68 Bo-Bo diesel electrics have proven to be very successful and reliable locomotives, highly capable in service, hauling passenger trains up to load 6, with good performance levels recorded on the latest high-tech diesel multiple units (DMU). The class is capable of hauling freight loads up to 2,000 tonnes, all within a relatively lightweight 86-tonne design. Designed to offer a stop-start system to reduce emissions and increased efficiency, the locomotives, with their attractive, modern curved styling and characteristic sounds have become popular with rail enthusiasts and train crews.

Vossloh had taken over the former Meinfesa (Mediterranea de Industries del Ferrocarril) Albuixech plant in Valencia, Spain, (owned by Alstom since 1991) on 1 January 2016. The plant had previously built a large number of Spanish locomotives, including Classes 310, 311 and 319, and more recently the EMD/Alstom Class 67s.

## UK EuroLight

Vossloh worked with Beacon Rail to design a version of its EuroLight train that would comply with the British loading gauge and crash worthiness regulations, together with British warning systems including automatic warning system (AWS) and train protection and warning system (TPWS). The UK EuroLight shares the loco family's general design as a diesel electric Bo-Bo with four AC traction motors, a lightweight monocoque body, ABB (ASEA Brown Boveri, formed in 1988 by the merger of Swiss Company Allmänna Svenska Elektriska

Aktiebolaget (ASEA) and the Swiss firm Brown, Boverie & Cie), AC transmission and Vossloh microprocessor control, all fitted within a narrower design that can be accommodated within the UK's restricted loading gauge. The prototype EuroLight loco (DB 248002) was displayed at the InnoTrans trade fair in Berlin in 2010, generating much interest from the railway media and industry. Versions of the EuroLight are now available for broad- or narrow-gauge railways, and a long distance 7,000-litre fuel capacity type is also included.

## Orders and production

The adoption of new emission limits for diesel locomotives by the European Union (stage IIIA up to 1 January 2012, stage IIIB afterwards) led to a rush to get the first batch of Class 68s built and delivered into the UK before the end of 2014. DRS announced its order placed with Stadler Rail (the new owner of Vossloh), for 15 160km/h (100mph) EuroLight locomotives for intermodal and passenger work on 5 January 2012, at a cost of €45m. The first loco would be outshopped in late 2013. The Total Operations Processing System (TOPS) designation of Class 68 was confirmed in February 2013.

Impressed with the first batch of locos received, DRS took up the option for a follow-on order for ten more in September 2014, followed by another seven in July 2015.

## Construction and testing

Construction of the Class 68 fleet began in May 2013 at Vossloh's Valencia Works in Albuixech, (Valencia) Spain – the same factory that built the Class 67 locomotives in 1999 while still part of the GEC-Alstom group.

68001 was the first of the type to be outshopped in all-over white livery with Vossloh branding. A three-month testing period began using this locomotive at the Velim test circuit from December 2013. The test programme included running in multiple with a EuroLight loco with trains loaded up to more than 2,000 tonnes. The EuroLight loco used serial 284001 (listed as both German and Italian Class 284

**68001 at Barrow Hill on 19 April 2015 at the 'Rarities' event. Around this time, few of the class had yet worked passenger services and interest from enthusiasts was high. The quarter mile length of 40k/ph (25mph) track didn't overly tax the new 3,800hp locomotive and the event was highly successful, with many seeing a Class 68 for the first time with very favourable feedback all round.**

## Introduction

and previously based at Kiel, a main site for Vossloh). 68001 was recorded on 11 February 2014 on the Velim test track, paired with 284001, with the 68 leading and powering a 20-car-long coal hopper train, during loaded performance testing. During the testing period, telemetry from the two EuroLight locomotives in service in Germany and Italy was also examined closely by DRS.

68001 was the first Class 68 to arrive in the UK, at Liverpool on 29 August 2014, though its stay was very brief, being transferred on to Berlin for display at the Innotrans 2014 tradeshow. It was returned to Valencia in early summer 2014 for minor modifications and repairs before receiving a full painting into DRS livery and being returned to the UK.

68002 was outshopped in full DRS livery and was tested in Spain, running on the Vossloh multi-gauge test track at Albuixech. It was formally presented to DRS Chief Executive Neil McNicholas at the Spanish plant on 16 December 2013. Upon completion, 68002 was shipped to Southampton and transported to Carlisle via Crewe in January 2014 – the first Class 68 for training and commissioning work in the UK. From 5 February 2014, it was tested for dynamic braking; hauled dead in a rake of 11 Mk 2 coaches and a Class 47 (90020); and run empty between Carlisle and Crewe Gresty Lane down the West Coast Main Line with the following trains:

12.54 5Z69 Carlisle–Crewe Gresty Green Up Loop
19.19 5Z70 Crewe Gresty Green Up Loop–Carlisle.

Locomotives 68003 and 68004 were completed in Valencia in March 2014 and shipped to Liverpool for onwards rail haulage to Crewe. In April 2014, 68005 *Defiant* was displayed at the National Exhibition Centre, Birmingham, at the Multimodal event held there.

**68027 on its second day in revenue-earning service, in 'plain blue', and before the *Splendid* nameplates were fitted, is seen at Milton (Brampton) on the Tyne Valley line heading west on the short-lived 6C89 10.51 Mountsorrel–Carlisle Yard Network Rail Supply Chain Operations bulk ballast flow on 3 May 2017. This and the equivalent Crewe working were utilised as 'heavy' loaded test runs for the locos when new, as was the case here. (Martin Taylor)**

68023 *Achilles* + 68002 *Intrepid* storm through Oxenholme on 26 March 2017 working 4M48, the Mossend to Daventry 'Tesco' container service in place of the more usual pair of 66s on this particular Sunday. The more common traction for this service, the bi-mode Class 88s, were still in the testing and acceptance stage at this point; the last five of the class of ten only being delivered just over a week before this photo was taken. (Martin Taylor)

The second batch of Class 68s was ordered in September 2014 (68016–68025), with the third order in July 2015 (68026–68032). Shortly afterwards, two more were ordered (68033 and 68034). From 68016 onwards, the locos were delivered by ship into Workington Port before being hauled the short distance to Carlisle Kingmoor TMD for full commissioning work to be carried out. 68016 and 68017 were unloaded from the cargo ship *DOUWE-S* on 26 October 2015 and transferred to Carlisle by sister loco 68004. They were delivered in base blue livery without numbers or insignia, leading to much speculation as to their use and ownership.

Another order for seven more locos (68026–68034) was signed on 28 July 2015, with this order signed by the new owner Stadler. The final two locos ordered (68033 and 68034) were funded directly by DRS and were delivered in July 2017.

There were rumours that DRS would order another batch of 10 or 13 locomotives, taking the fleet serial number up to 68044 or 68047. Instead, the company selected Class 88s, ordering ten dual-mode locomotives, utilising the same bodyshell, with only the number and shape of bodyside grilles being different from the diesel-only Class 68s.

Pending the arrival of its new fleet of Class 68s, DRS constructed a purpose-built shed at Crewe Gresty Bridge to house the locos, and on 11 March 2014, DRS displayed 68002 to the press there.

Class 68 servicing was designed to be simpler than standard practice, with regular and organised intervals of minor servicing at 1,000 hours (including exams up to an oil change) and major servicing at 18,000 hours (top-end overhaul). The new facility accommodated test and warranty engineers from Vossloh, ABB and Caterpillar.

DRS sent 57007 to collect the last three Class 68s built. 68034, 68032 and 68033. Delivered aboard the 2014-built Dutch-registered cargoship *Eemslift Ellen* to Workington Docks, and unloaded the same morning, the locos were given a quick fitness to run (FTR) exam on the quayside, then moved to their new home for commissioning as 0Z17 12.10 Workington Docks–Kingmoor Depot, seen here east of Wigton on 24 July 2017. A layer of dust from their time in transit is evident on the tops of the locos. 57007 had previously had the honour of collecting 68012, 68013 and 68014 on delivery from Liverpool Gladstone Dock–Kingmoor on 29 August 2014. (Martin Taylor)

The family lines are clearly evident with bi-mode Class 88 88008 at Cathiron on 26 July 2020 working the Sunday afternoon 4S45 15.15 Daventry–Mossend 'Tesco' liner service; the loco clearly bearing a great similarity to its Class 68 cousins.

## Teething troubles

For such a revolutionary new design of locomotive, the introduction of the Class 68 fleet was relatively trouble free with only minor delays, mostly due to training, paperwork and certification issues, or problems with the rolling stock being used, notably CAF Mk 5As.

The biggest mechanical problem to date with the Class 68 was revealed on 28 June 2021, when a DRS press release confirmed it had removed 13 of 34 locomotives from traffic after discovering a small crack in a bracket around an electrical cubicle during a routine inspection. The defect was corrected over the course of the next few months with DRS emphasising that there had been no risk to the safety of staff, passengers or the general public at any time.

On 23 October 2015, 68015 suffered a serious turbocharger fire at High Wycombe while working 1G25, the 10.45 Marylebone–Birmingham Snow Hill. The fire was suppressed by the 68's on-board foam system, but four fire engines were dispatched to the scene and the following day the loco was dragged from Wembley to Crewe by 68002 for assessment and repair. 68011 suffered a similar fire. DRS identified the cause of the fires on 68011 and 68015 as sound baffles disintegrating in the exhaust and causing turbo fires. 68001–007 were the first of the fleet to be modified to prevent this. Both 68011 and 68015 locomotives were repaired at the DRS facility at Longport; the site having been previously used for minor modifications on some of the locomotives after their arrival from Spain.

**On 21 April 2022, 68015 arrives at Smethwick Galton Bridge (High Level Station) on 1H17, the 06.41 Stourbridge Junction to London Marylebone.**

# Chapter 1
# Technical Specifications

The Class 68s are very advanced state-of-the-art diesel electrics, rated at 3,800hp with a wide range of electronic control and analytical systems, together with innovative fuel economy, reliability and ease of maintenance features. The overall value of DRS's first batch contract with Vossloh and Beacon Rail was thought to be £45m (around £3m per loco, though later reports quoted a cost of £5.4m each).

Pending delivery of the new Class 93s and 99s in the near future, the Class 68s are still the only currently available mainline diesel locomotives that can be easily adapted to comply with the strict Stage IIIB emission limits (though older locomotives in the UK can be fitted with IIIA compliant power units under 'grandfather' rights). Under EU emissions rulings, only 26 new-build Stage IIIA-compliant locomotives could be ordered before the 31 December 2014 deadline, comprising 16 for Europe-wide operators and 10 specifically for the UK. Some space would be needed for additional equipment to convert the C175-16 engine for Stage IIIB compliance (replacing the exhaust silencer with a diesel particulate filter), meaning that follow-on orders for Class 68s would require a substantial redesign.

The Class 68 functions are controlled by an onboard computer control system (TCMS). The system controls tractive effort (anti-slide protection), dynamic braking and Emissions Trading System (ETS) supply, together with auxiliary functions such as sanding, cooling, auxiliary loads and start up.

On 3 December 2022, 68011 awaits departure from London Marylebone on 1R24, the 11.00 to Birmingham Moor Street, as the driver makes final preparations. The Class 68 cab is an advanced design, built around an ergonomic single central driving position. See the annotated photo on page 15 for a full description of the controls.

Class 68s also have two sets of telemetry equipment for performance analysis and fault reporting. The TCMS detects and warns of most fault conditions giving audible warnings and visual displays on the train management display in each cab with downloadable logs.

## Speeding and braking

Overspeed protection is controlled by TCMS with traction output cutting out at 165km/h (102.5mph) and emergency braking applied at 172km/h (107mph). At this point, an alarm bell sounds and a screen message displays "NO TRACTION – OVERSPEED DETECTED", or "EMERGENCY BRAKE APPLIED – OVERSPEED DETECTED". In the first instance, power can be reapplied after speed drops to 155km/h (96mph). In an emergency-stop situation the loco will be brought down to below 2km/h (1/4mph) by emergency braking.

The Class 68 is fitted with a complex braking system with multiple options and combinations including:

### *Automatic brake with blending*

A Class 68 running light engine will use the blending brake as the main brake to apply brake effort. In service, the hauled stock or wagons will brake using the pressure of the brake pipe (BP), independently of the brake mode chosen in the locomotive. The service brake with blending consists of a dynamic brake in the locomotive and in the train through the automatic BP. This is applied by actuating the automatic brake handle on the desk.

### *Automatic brake without blending*

The service brake without blending is a pneumatic brake with adjustable braking and releasing that actuates in the locomotive and in the train through an automatic BP. This is applied through the brake valve on the driving desk by the automatic brake handle.

### *Direct brake*

The direct brake (electro-pneumatic) only applies in the locomotive and is actuated via the direct brake handle on the cab desk.

### *Parking brake*

The loco's parking brake is a passive spring-accumulated brake (increasing effort with decreasing air pressure). The brake is released by applying air pressure to the parking cylinder to resist the pressure exerted by the accumulating spring.

### *Rheostatic electric brake (dynamic brake)*

The locomotive electric brake is a rheostatic type with traction motor energy transformed into heat through the dynamic brake grids. This brake is applied by using the power brake controller, in the brake position. It is possible to operate the automatic brake in a combined way with the electric brake, by applying the electric brake in the locomotive and the pneumatic brake in the train. The electric brake operation cancels the locomotive pneumatic brake, if applied.

### *Back-up brake (service auxiliary brake)*

The back-up brake system pneumatically controls the BPs through the direct brake handle. It is only used in the unlikely event of the automatic brake failing. In this mode the direct brake is not operative.

For locomotive automatic braking, there are eight-disc brake units located on each wheel, with an automatically adjusted stroke.

On 21 January 2023, with the imposing tower of the Kirklees' Incinerator as a backdrop, 68034 arrives into Huddersfield with 1U52, the 13.12 Malton–Manchester Piccadilly. The service started at Malton on this day due to an unusual mid-week engineering blockade between there and Scarborough.

On 11 November 2022, 68034 shoves 1F72, the 15.34 Scarborough–Manchester, out of the magnificent York station on its way on the only regular daily westwards loco-hauled service, at that time, over the Pennines, helping to maintain TPE train crew's traction and route knowledge in advance of the reintroduction of a more intensive loco-hauled service from the December 2022 timetable change.

|    | Operating mode     | Action          | Result                                                     |
|----|--------------------|-----------------|------------------------------------------------------------|
| 1  | Power              | Dynamic brake   | Traction cut out (Combined power/brake lever)              |
| 2  | Power              | Automatic brake | Blending (loco)/Pneumatic (train)                          |
| 3  | Power              | Emergency brake | Emergency braking                                          |
| 4  | Power              | Direct brake    | Direct brake in loco (and power off if above 5km/h/3mph)   |
| 5  | Dynamic brake      | Power           | Traction cut out (same lever operates both)                |
| 6  | Dynamic brake      | Automatic brake | Blending in loco/automatic brake in train                  |
| 7  | Dynamic brake      | Emergency brake | Emergency braking                                          |
| 8  | Dynamic brake      | Direct brake    | Dynamic brake only                                         |
| 9  | Dynamic brake      | Power           | Traction cut out (same lever operates both)                |
| 10 | Automatic brake    | Emergency brake | Emergency braking                                          |
| 11 | Automatic brake    | Direct brake    | Stronger pneumatic brake will apply to the loco            |
| 12 | Applied emergency  | Any other action| Emergency braking                                          |
| 13 | Direct brake       | Power           | See 4 above                                                |
| 14 | Direct brake       | Automatic brake | Stronger pneumatic brake will apply to the loco            |
| 15 | Direct brake       | Applied emergency | Emergency braking                                        |
| 16 | Direct brake       | Dynamic brake   | See 8 above                                                |
| 17 | Power/Dynamic brake| Parking brake   | Cut out of power/Dynamic brake                             |
| 18 | Back-up brake      | Direct brake    | Not possible (combined lever)                              |

## Driving cab

The driving cabs have been designed in accordance with UIC 651 OR Standard and are high stiffness steel structures with fibreglass reinforced fairings for maximum energy absorbance. Insulating material and fibreglass-reinforced polyester protect against heat and noise, with additional insulation at the cab rear provided by rock wool and fire-resistant felt.

Maintenance access is simplified by the use of three removable roof hatches for the electric room, power unit and cooling system.

- Electric room hatch – with dynamic brake grids and the main air reservoirs. This hatch is above the clean air section and the air inlet filters are mounted in both sides of the car body.
- Diesel engine hatch provided with a diesel exhaust silencer.
- Cooling system hatch, featuring the radiators fans and compensating tank of the diesel engine cooling circuit.

## Environment

To help protect the track and environment, a 190-litre (42-gallon) retention tank is linked to the fuel tank. The tank collects residues (oil, water, fuel) that fall into the main generator tray and prevents them from falling on the track. The retention tank needs to be drained as part of scheduled maintenance.

## Technical Specifications

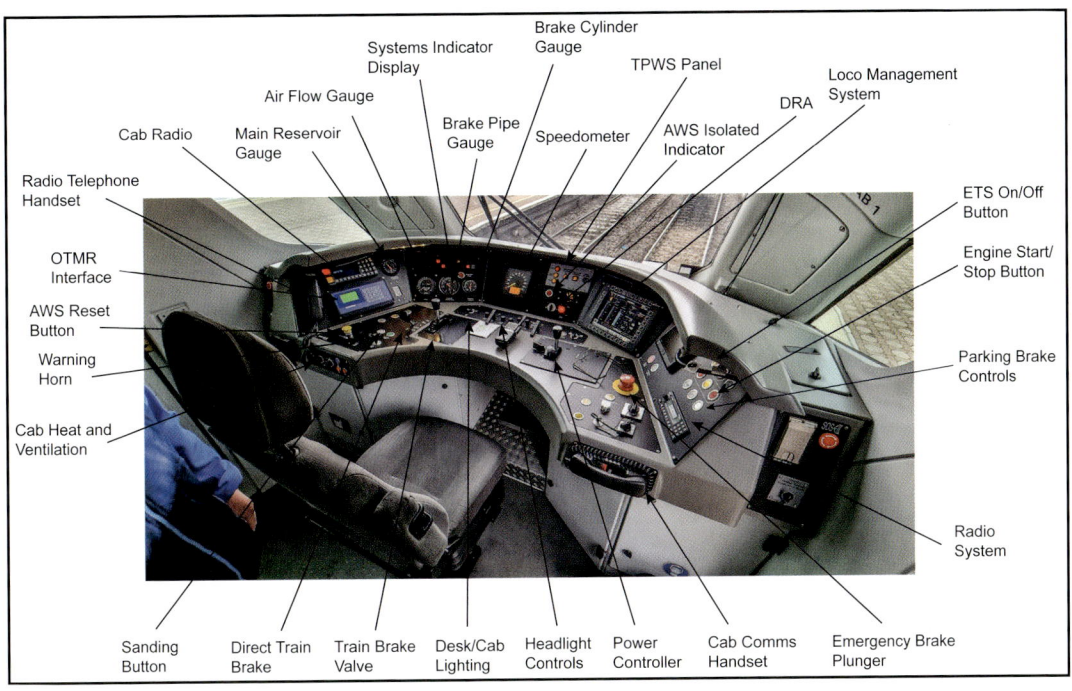

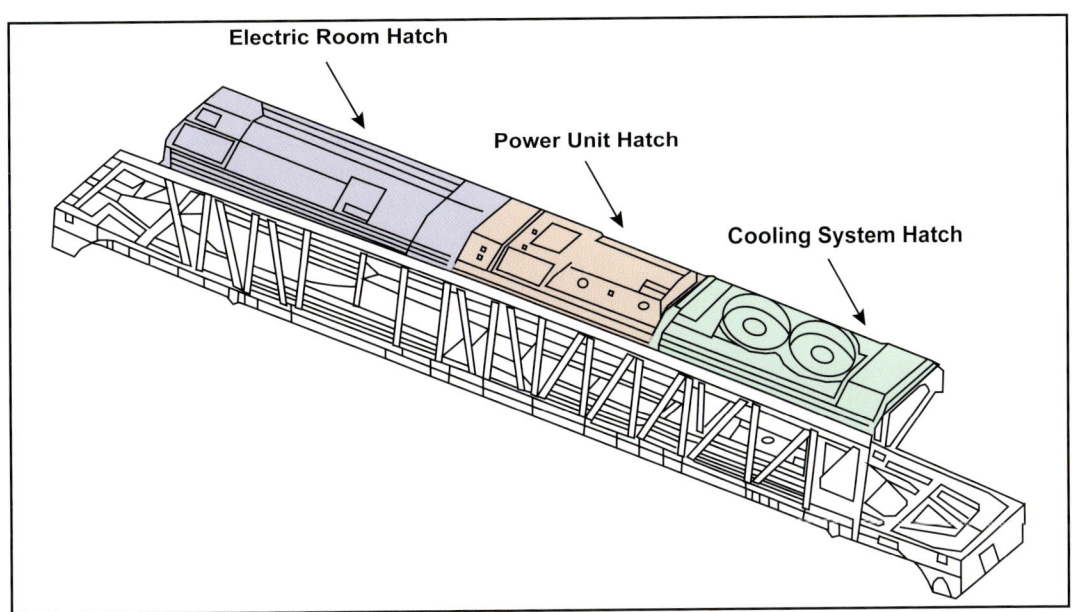

## Power

Class 68s can operate in multiple (within Class) and also with the Class 88s. In addition, where the loco is Association of American Railroads (AAR) multiple unit (MU) system fitted and in push-pull mode with a driver van trailer (DVT). AAR control is required for push-pull working on passenger duties. Fitting of AAR equipment involves extensive rewiring and remodelling of the cab arrangements and is unlikely to be retrofitted to any of the first batch of locos.

The Chiltern DVTs operated with the Class 68-hauled Mk 3 services between Birmingham and London Marylebone had previously been modified to work with Class 67s (initially hired to haul the services) by adding a notched power controller, and having extra diesel generators to enable electric train service (ETS) supply when the loco is switched off.

The CAT C175-16 ACERTTM power unit is a member of Caterpillar's successful C175 series of 16-cylinder and 20-cylinder engines, used mainly in heavy earth-moving equipment, oil rigs and generator sets. The power unit is capable of an output of up to 4,700hp, giving a generated output of up

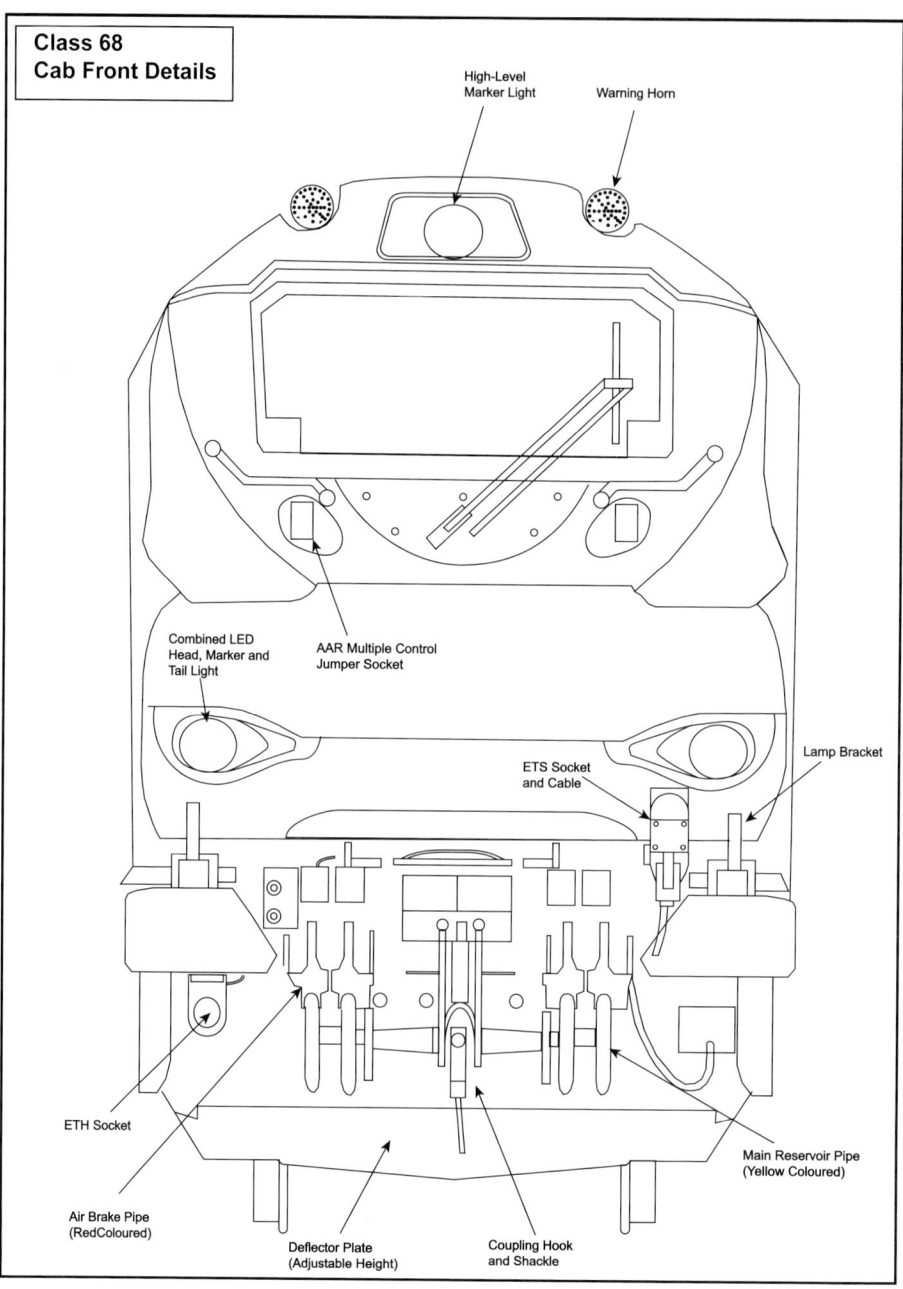

## Technical Specifications

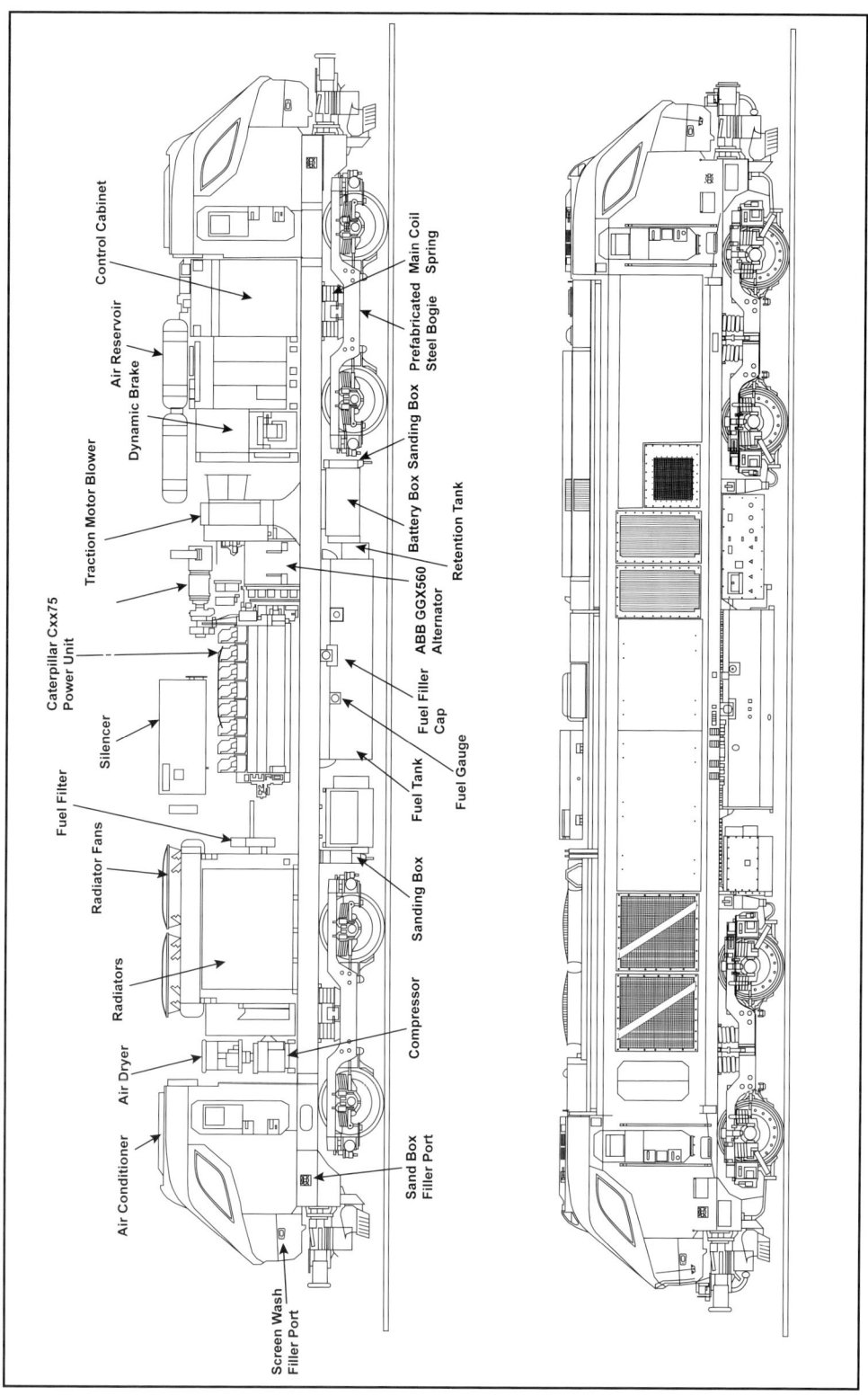

to 4MW (enough to power up to 400 homes). One CAT C175 diesel generator set is currently powering the whole of the holiday island of Mustique.

The C175 has also been installed in locomotives elsewhere including the European EuroLight locos. In the US, C175s are found in Progress Rail's PR43C (a conversion of an EMD-powered SD50 freight loco), and EMD's F125 *Spirit*, a four-axle, 200km/h (125mph) passenger diesel locomotive, which is powered by a Caterpillar C175-20 diesel engine rated at 4,700hp (3,500kW) and which was ordered for the Los Angeles commuter agency Metrolink. The Class 68 is, however, the first use of a CAT 175 in a British locomotive.

When coupled to Mk 3 or Mk 5 stock for working passenger trains in push-pull mode (the usual working arrangement, the No.2 end of the loco is almost always coupled next to the stock. Exceptions include working excursions/railtours, or (previously) when hauling Mk 2 stock in East Anglia, the Fife Circle or Cumbria. The reason for this is because the No.1 cab is where the main DVT/Loco driving mode switch is located (in a compartment behind the cab) – preventing delays and a noisy walk through the engine compartment when reversing the train at termini. Additionally, the No.2 end of a Class 68 contains the air brake compressor, making the No.2 cab much noisier. By placing this next to the coaching stock the loco will always be driven from the quieter No.1 cab, or the DVT.

Compared to the standard EuroLight locos, the UK Light version has a higher top speed, due to different gearing (increased to160km/h/100mph from 140km/h/86mph), a narrower profile – to fit in the UK's loading gauge and with a fuel tank enlarged from 4,000l to 5,000l.

To increase efficiency, the power unit is fitted with automatic stop-start technology and will shut down after a period of idling, such as at a signal stop. A manual override facility is also available, and the loco will re-start if coolant temperature falls below a certain level. On shed, the loco can be fitted to a ground supply, which provides 415V 3-phase AC to maintain coolant temperature, cab heating and demisters.

Caterpillar worked with ABB to reduce the weight of the power unit and alternator set for UK use, with an ABB alternator specifically designed for use with the C175 engine and bolted directly to it. Parts of the engine/alternator set have been designed in aluminium in order to save weight, bringing the 68's power unit down to 11 tonnes compared to 12 tonnes with a standard C175.

The ABB WGX560 6-pole 3-phase brushless alternator is directly coupled to the engine. This supplies two traction packages (ABB Boardline CC1500 DE Compact Converters) with rectifiers for DC supply for ETS and dynamic braking. Class 68 drive electronics (AC800 PEC) features adhesion control (anti-slip), with automatic sanding.

## Traction control

ABB, working together with Vossloh España, produced a traction control package that ensured that the strong, but lightly axle-loaded EuroLight and Class 68 Bo-Bos are able to transfer as much of their installed power into tractive effort at the rail surface as possible. Vossloh was involved in the design of the traction package from an early stage and had input into the synchronous (AC) generator, a pair of BORDLINE CC1500 DE traction converters all coupled to four traction motors. Each traction motor is supplied by an individual motor inverter to ensure maximum adhesion control. The BORDLINE CC1500 DE traction convertor is an Insulated-Gate Bipolar Transistor type (IGBT) type – a semiconductor fast electronic switch, similar to thyristors, which includes water-cooled Power Electronic Building Blocks (PEBBs) – rectifiers, two motor convertors, a braking chopper and an auxiliary convertor for internal locomotive auxiliary systems.

The passenger traction package also includes a BORDLINE M500 head-end power supply. The unit supplies two 900V DC outputs from the three-phase AC input. The Class 68 and other passenger versions of the EuroLight also include an extra PEBB to feed this BORDLINE M500 hep unit.

The ABB 2.8 MVA brushless (synchronous) air-cooled single-bearing generator is coupled directly to the Caterpillar power unit. Weight-saving materials and design advances have enabled the generator

## Technical Specifications

to be delivered tipping the scales at only 5.3 tonnes. The generator is a self-excited type coupled to an automatic voltage regulator – the UNITROL 1010 (also produced by ABB).

Class 68 bogies are a standard gauge version of those used on the Spanish (RENFE) Class 334 (Vossloh Euro 3000) high-speed diesel electric locos with Primary and Secondary suspension provided by means of coil springs. Traction power is distributed by traction inverters supplying four AC traction motors fitted to the bogies and directly geared to the wheels.

*Above*: 68008 *Avenger*, upon arrival at Birmingham Snow Hill, after another excellent run from London on 16 May 2015 with 1K54, the 18.15 Marylebone–Kidderminster.

*Right*: On 19 July 2016, 68010 approaches Hatton on 1K45, the 16.45 London Marylebone–Kidderminster.

Convertor control is via the AC800 PEC platform – used in all ABB traction convertors to maintain optimum power management, energy efficiency and ultimately maximizing adhesion. The whole package has an ethernet link to enable an interface with BORDLINE View diagnostics software

The ABB AMXL400 frame mounted traction motors are of the six-pole AC induction type with open force ventilation cooling and a weight of only 1.85 tonnes – separate electronic control for each axle ensures maximum adhesion capability.

## Lights

Some concern was voiced that the headlights on the class are too bright for drivers of passing trains, particularly at night or in tunnels, though inquiries with the Rail Safety and Standards Board concluded that this was not an issue and reaffirmed that they complied with Group Standards.

## Builder's plates

As with most modern locomotives, the builder's plates on the Class 68s are made of etched brushed aluminium, applied along the bodysides and below the driver's position. 68001 to 68025 have Vossloh plates and the remainder are fitted with Stadler ones, reflecting the change in ownership as the supply contract was fulfilled. Other differences between the two plate types are font types and the addition of the assembly plant (Valencia) on the Stadler plates.

## DRS Class 68 orders

**Batch 1**  15 locos (68001–68015) ordered on 19 January 2015, and delivered 2013–14.
**Batch 2**  10 locos (68016–68025) ordered on 11 September 2014, with delivery between October 2015 and February 2016 at a rate of two per month.
**Batch 3**  Seven locos (68026–68032), ordered July 2015, with delivery at the end of 2016.

### Technical specification for Class 68 locomotive

| | |
|---|---|
| Numbers | 68001–68032 |
| Wheel arrangement | Bo-Bo |
| Length over buffers | 20.5m (67ft 3in) |
| Width | 2.69m (8ft 10in) |
| Height on new wheelsets | 3.82m (12ft 6in) |
| Wheelbase | 2.80m (9ft 2in) |
| Bogie wheelbase | 2.80m (9ft 2in) |
| Bogie pivot centres | 11.83m (38ft 8in) |
| Wheel diameter (new) | 1.1m (3ft 7in) |
| Wheel diameter (maximum wear) | 1.02m (3ft 4in) |
| Weight (maximum) | 86 tonnes |
| Axle load | 21.5 tonnes per axle |
| Route availability | Seven |
| Minimum curve radius (mainline) | 250m (273 yards) |
| Minimum curve radius (dead slow) | 80m (88 yards) |

| | |
|---|---|
| Maximum speed | 160km/h (100mph) |
| Starting tractive effort | 317kN (71,264lbf) |
| Continuous tractive effort | 56,200lbf (250kN) |
| Fuel capacity | 5,000 litres (1,100 gallons) stored in a high-impact resistance tank made of welded aluminum and fitted with baffles |
| Engine oil | 509 litres (112 gallons) |
| Cooling water | 900 litres (198 gallons) |
| Sand | 360 litres (79 gallons) – pneumatic |
| Power unit | Caterpillar C175 – V16 4 stroke of 2800kW (3,750hp) at 1,740rpm |
| Power unit weight | Approximately 11,500kg (11.3 tons) |
| Injection system | Common rail electronic unit injection |
| Turbocharger | Four free-wheeling turbochargers |
| Idle speed | 600 rpm |
| Maximum speed | 1800 rpm |
| Power at rail | 2,380kW (3,190hp) |
| Multiple working | Within class and Class 88s only; maximum two locomotives |
| Cylinder bore | 175mm 96.9in) |
| Cylinder stroke | 220mm (8.7in) |
| Main alternator | ABB – WGX560PB6 – 6-pole brushless of 2760kW at 1,740rpm single bearing, self-excited synchronous alternator |
| Alternator weight | Approximately 5,200kg |
| Rectifiers | Two ABB Bordline CC1500 DE compact converter/rectifier packs |
| Traction motors | Four ABB – AMXL400FAIME1CF06 of 600kW (804.6hp) at 725rpm |
| Gear ratio | 4:52 |
| ETS | 500kW – Index 96 |
| Pneumatic brake | KNORR – MBS with anti-skid |
| Brake types | EP, Air Disc, Dynamic, Regenerative |
| Compressor | KNORR – MBS SL20-5 |
| Bodyshell | Monocoque, carbon steel / high strength steel and oxidation-resistant steel (copper steel) |
| Bogie type | Vossloh Bo-Bo (fabricated) |
| Electronic maintenance | Remote telemetry to DRS control offering real time condition monitoring |
| Batteries | Lead-acid four batteries of 12V connected in two series x two parallel Nominal Voltage. 24V Capacity (amps per hour). 2 x 175 Ah Start Battery (is used only for starting diesel power unit) |
| Pneumatic brake type | KNORR-MBS disc brake cylinders |
| Maximum pressure in brake cylinders | 3,6 bar (52.2lbs per square inch) |
| Anti-skid system | Fitted |
| Compressed air assembly | KNORR-MBS SL20-5 (Twin-shaft rotary compressor) |
| Suspension, Primary | Coil springs |
| Suspension, Secondary | Coil springs. Vertical and horizontal dampers |
| Brake effort | 165kN (37,100lbf) (max), 45kN (10,100lbf) at 160km/h (100mph) |
| Brake force | 65.2 tonnes |
| Owners | 68001–68032 Beacon Rail; 68033–68034 DRS |

## Performance and use

DRS has been very impressed with the performance of its new locomotives in terms of reliability and haulage capabilities. The loco represents an advance over the older Class 67 in terms of power output, fuel efficiency and axle loading. Chiltern was keen to make use of the new class as quickly as possible to help further accelerate services and also with a view to increasing train lengths on its routes.

Other advantages of the new locos include greater fuel efficiency (anecdotal evidence from maintenance staff originally stated it to be 7 per cent higher than similar horsepower EMD power units, but Chiltern stated this is even higher, in the range of 10 per cent). The large fuel tank (5,600 litres/1210 gallons) also gives a wide operating range.

Other noted improvements over older locomotives such as the Class 67s, include cleaner exhaust, minimised maintenance, greater reliability, remote telemetry and diagnostics and regenerative braking.

The class has earned wide-ranging plaudits for its performance on passenger and freight services with the gearing of the locomotive for 160km/h (100mph) running allowing impressive acceleration, rivalling that of multiple units, a great advantage in terms of diagramming and pathing of Class 68-hauled services. In freight service, the loco can comfortably haul a 1,600-tonne intermodal load or 2,000-tonne ballast train. Vossloh also offered the option for reconfiguring the top speed of the loco to 200km/h (125mph) running.

DRS crews have confirmed that when running light engine, the locos can accelerate up to 96km/h (60mph) from a standing start in less than 20 seconds, a performance comparable to some older models of family saloon cars. On heavier loads, a Class 68 on a charter service, with a trailing load of 11 Mk 1s, managed a speed of 93km/h (58mph) at the top of the Lickey Incline (the steepest incline in the UK rail network), compared to a speed of 61km/h (38mph) achieved by a Deltic hauling the same load.

The Class 68s in service have been relatively fault-free, though there were delays to their initial introduction into service due to TPWS problems and overloading of the motor alternator sets in Mk 3 sets due to ETS issues. Any failures in service are largely due to problems with the ageing Mk 3s on Chiltern or the Mk 5a CAF stock on Trans Pennine Express (TPE) services.

## Speed

68002 *Intrepid* began test-running with a rake of 11 Mk 2 coaches, hauled dead inside by Class 47 47853 between Carlisle Kingmoor and Carlisle, with 90020 forward to Crewe Gresty Lane, testing starting on 4 February 2014. As part of their testing for suitability for Chiltern services, one of the stated performance characteristics was that the 68s would be able to match the timings for six-car Class 168 'Clubman' diesel multiple units (DMU) – the fastest timed traction on the line between Kidderminster and London Marylebone.

Sources state that this was achieved with a margin to spare. A 68 hauling a Chiltern load of six Mk 3s and a driving van trailer (DVT) has been logged accelerating its train up to 80km/h (50mph) within one minute, outperforming DMUs on the route, including the new Class 172s. The test runs showed that the 68s could match the DMUs in terms of acceleration, braking and maintaining their designed maximum speed, thereby ensuring that existing start-to-stop timings could be retained upon the introduction of Class 68 hauled services and that the timetable wouldn't need to be recast to allow for slower trains. The performance also means that Class 168 DMUs could substitute on booked Class 68 hauled services (and vice versa).

Experience shows that, while accelerating, the 68s are generally around 16km/h (10mph) faster through most passing points, compared to the previous traction. The only driver complaints (that the author has heard of) regarding Class 68s are due to the amount of power available. They are prone to wheelslip, even at three-figure speeds.

The Class 68s have also garnered praise from railtour operators for their excellent performance (enabling tours to be pathed easily over high-speed main lines). Insiders have confirmed that the class

## Technical Specifications

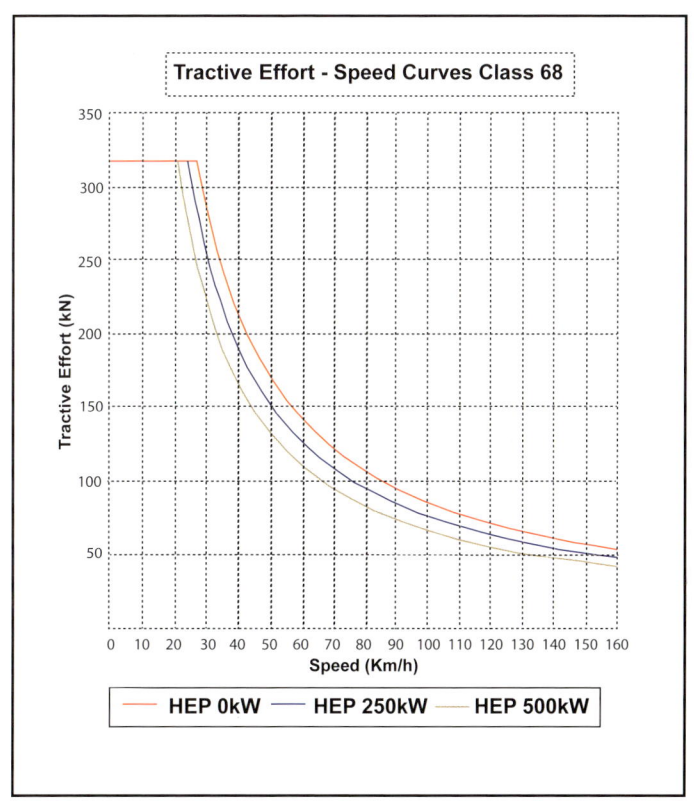

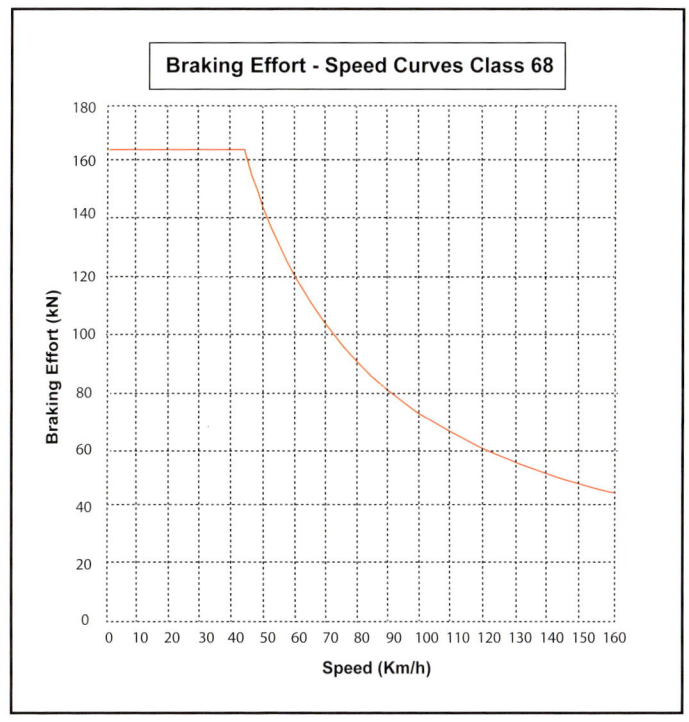

On 2 November 2019, 68008 *Avenger* stands at London Marylebone with 1K50, the 17.00 to Kidderminster. In the adjoining platform, 168219 (one of the later 168/2 subclass) stands with the empties from an earlier arrival from Birmingham.

On the morning of 21 April 2022, 68013 *Peter Wreford-Bush* shoves 1H22, the 07.16 Stourbridge Junction to London Marylebone, away from Smethwick Galton Bridge (High Level).

*Right*: On 9 December 2022, 68011 propels 1H45, the 12.55 Birmingham Moor Street–London Marylebone, away from High Wycombe.

*Below*: 68005 *Defiant* draws the empty stock of a railtour from Leeds via Canterbury into the sidings, with 68018 *Vigilant* at the rear.

is able to keep to within one minute or equal for Class 86/87 timings between London King's Cross and Peterborough, with loads up to 12 or 13 coaches.

While the trains are crewed by Chiltern staff, DRS is responsible for much of the maintenance of the Class 68s with staff present on site at Wembley Depot, and major works taking place at its main Crewe depot.

**On Saturday 15 December 2019, 68008** *Avenger* **stands at an almost empty London Marylebone with 1K50, the 17.00 to Kidderminster.**

**68014, in its new low-emission fuel livery, departs Bicester North with 1H45, the 12.45 Birmingham Moor Street to London Marylebone service on 26 May 2023.**

On 17 August 2019, 68011 propels 1H45, the 12.55 Birmingham Moor Street–London Marylebone, away from High Wycombe. The high power of the Class 68 leads to strong heat haze effects from the exhausts, more pronounced when using telephotos – as is the case here. This image was taken with a 500mm prime lens.

68014 passes Fenny Compton (between Leamington Spa and Banbury) on 17 July 2017 working 1H69, the 15.55 Birmingham Moor Street–London Marylebone.

# Chapter 2
# Chiltern Railways

Chiltern Railways had originally introduced loco-hauled services over its route in 2010, utilising a slam-door set of Mk 3s hauled by a DB Schenker Class 67 on hire. Previously, starting in April 2008, a loco-hauled service had operated over the route (from Wrexham to London Marylebone, calling at Tame Bridge Parkway), though its operator ceased business in January 2011, with Chiltern (also owned by DB Regio) taking the opportunity to purchase the defunct sister company's recently refurbished four rakes of Mk 3s for further use, together with the Class 67s on hire from DB.

Chiltern Railways announced, in April 2014, that it would lease six Class 68s from DRS, at a cost of £15m, to replace its Class 67 fleet on services out of London Marylebone, with the contract for lease beginning in December that year. However, the lease for the rail operator's existing 67s was extended to May 2015, as not enough Class 68s would be ready for the planned December takeover – around 110 drivers needed to be fully trained or have conversion courses to the Class 68s and not enough locomotives could be made available until October 2014.

On 5 August 2014, 68002 made a debut for the class over the Chiltern Main Line, running light engine after conducting noise testing on shed at Stourbridge Junction in advance of them being stabled there overnight for use on London Marylebone services (testing for ambient noise that may have disturbed the peace of local residents). The first loaded test run for Chiltern-liveried Class 68s took place on 20 August 2014, when 68010 and 68011 hauled an empty rake of Mk 2 coaches southwards through Carlisle. This was followed by the first passenger working on the Chiltern route.

A dedicated fleet of Chiltern two-tone silver and grey Class 68s (68010–68015) was allocated for use on the services into and out of London Marylebone, with DRS-liveried Class 68008 and 68009 also available for hire at times of shortages. These two locos having been fitted with the required AAR multiple working equipment to work with the Mk 2 DVTs used on the services in push-pull mode – visible as extra jumper connections above the buffer beams. The first Chiltern Class 68 workings took place on 15 December 2014, with 68012 on the 07.44 Banbury–London Marylebone and the 17.50 London Marylebone–Banbury route hauling Chiltern's slam-door Mk 3 set.

The Class 68 fleet finally took over all Chiltern Railways loco-hauled workings from DB Schenker Class 67s in May 2015, with 67008, 67013, and 67014 removed from the dedicated weighted average cost of capital (WACC) (DB Cargo UK Chiltern Hire CE Class 67) pool; the pool code then being redundant, though it is still on the system. The last 67 working recorded was 67014 on 27 May working 1R55, the 16.47 London Marylebone–Birmingham Moor Street, then returning the empties south as 5E90, the 19.40 Birmingham Moor Street–Wembley LMD.

The following day, 28 May 2015, was the first day of exclusively Class 68 haulage on Chiltern silver sets and featured 68008, 68010, 68011, 68013 and 68014 on the five loco-hauled diagrams.

On 16 February 2015, 68008 *Avenger* became the first DRS-liveried Class 68 to work a Chiltern passenger service when it propelled 1H20, the 07.44 Banbury–Marylebone into London.

On 25 October 2015, Chiltern began a new service from London Marylebone to Oxford Parkway (via a new chord at Bicester and calling at the rebuilt stations at Bicester Village, formerly Bicester Town and Islip). On the first day, 68014 was provided with a Mk 3 set to work the 11.45 from Oxford Parkway to London Marylebone.

On 9 December 2022, 68011 propels 1H45, the 12.55 Birmingham Moor Street–London Marylebone, away from High Wycombe.

On 13 July 2019, 68008 *Avenger* waits at a strangely deserted London Marylebone with 1R37, the 14.10 service to Birmingham Moor Street

68008 *Avenger* departs Haddenham and Thame Parkway on 1H45, the 12.55 from Birmingham Moor Street on 19 April 2022, propelling the train at high speed towards the capital.

On Sunday 25 October, the day before the timetabled opening of the new Chiltern route through to Oxford, 68014 had also worked two return specials along the route, including 1T23, the 10.35 Marylebone–Oxford Parkway. Class 68-hauled services with Chiltern to and from Oxford ended at the timetable change in December 2022.

Class 68s on the Chiltern services are unlikely to continue for many more years, with 2024 anticipated to be the final year of loco-hauled operations on the route – the hauled sets have had a number of stays of executions so far, with the Class 68s sub-leased to Chiltern from DRS on a rolling six-month basis. A number of issues have beset the use of loco-hauled services, including complaints regarding noise in the Marylebone area (with the local authority getting involved and instructions to shut down the locos in the station area and use the DVTs to supply electric train heating (ETH) whenever possible). Other issues have included high track access charges (when compared to the Class 168s), and also the increasing age, unreliability and cost of maintaining the Mk 3 sets.

Chiltern's Class 68s rarely venture off the operator's main Kidderminster to London Marylebone route, with little option for diversions. Two Chiltern loco-hauled sets have visited Stratford-upon-Avon, firstly on 4 November 2018 when 68010 worked 1D27, the 11.40 from London Marylebone and 1H37, 13.50 return to Marylebone. Disruption to the timetable on 9 November, saw 68015 reach Stratford on a diverted down service from London Marylebone, the loco then taking the empties back to Kidderminster.

Only on rare occasions have Class 68s other than 68008 to 68015 been used with Chiltern trains, the most famous occasion being a period starting on 10 February 2017, when 68002 and 68018 were hired from DRS at a time of severe locomotive shortage in the allocated fleet (due to faulty springs being found, necessitating a quick replacement programme carried out with each loco needing lifting on shed at Crewe or Kingmoor). 68002 and 68018 worked top-and-tail on the one remaining slam-door

On 18 January 2023, 68013 *Peter Wreford-Bush* stands ready to propel 1H53, the 14.55 departure southwards to London Marylebone, in the fading winter light.

68013 *Peter Wreford-Bush* propels 1H53, the 14.55 Birmingham Moor Street–London Marylebone, away from Banbury on 20 April 2022.

Class 68 68011 pauses at Dorridge on 3 December 2022, on 1R25, the 11.10 London Marylebone–Birmingham Moor Street.

Under a threatening sky, on 10 December 2022, 68013 shoves 1H45, the 15.37 Birmingham Moor Street–London Marylebone, into Leamington Spa.

Oxford Parkway station, on the line from Oxford to Bicester, was officially opened on Sunday 25 October 2015, and three days later 68008 arrived there with a train from London Marylebone. Through services from London Marylebone to Oxford began on 11 December 2016. At this time, just two-up and one-down Class 68-hauled commuter services were operated; in the morning 1Y12, the 07.24 Oxford Parkway–London Marylebone, and in the evening 1Y75, the 19.29 to London. In the other direction there was an 18.18 departure from London–Oxford Parkway, 1T54 – the train pictured here.

On 13 April 2022, Leamington was briefly host to three different Class 68s. 68013 in Bay Platform Number 1, being named *Peter Wreford-Bush* 68008 *Avenger* on 1H45, the 12.55 Birmingham Moor Street to London Marylebone, departs from Leamington Spa while 68015 arrives on 1R93, the 12.10 London Marylebone to Birmingham Moor Street.

*Left*: 68015 *Kev Helmer* arrives at Warwick Parkway on 18 March 2022, on 1R93, the 12.10 London Marylebone–Birmingham Moor Street. The station, north of the town of Warwick, is handily close to the A46 road, leading on to the M40. The station was opened on 25 October 2000 and is served by Chiltern Trains services.

*Below*: Following a brief but violent snow shower on 28 February 2018, unnamed 68013 propels 1H45, the 12.55 Birmingham Moor Street to London Marylebone, into Leamington Spa.

68014 arrives at Princes Risborough on 2 April 2022, working 1R32, the 13.00 London Marylebone–Birmingham Moor Street service. The stabling and run-round sidings for the Chinnor and Princes Risborough Railway can be seen in the background, the preserved line sharing a platform with the mainline Chiltern service here.

68011 pauses at Leamington Spa on 20 December 2016, working 1H69, the 15.55 Birmingham Moor Street–London Marylebone. One day before the shortest day of the year, the low light provides a rare opportunity for a night shot of a Class 68 at Leamington Spa; the later (down) trains being too far down the platform to photograph from the shorter up-platform.

Mk 3 set (AL05), due to the two locomotives not being compatible with the DVT for through multiple working. 68018 was attached to the up (south) end of the stock – coupled to the DVT (82309). Services worked included 1H06, the 06.23 Bicester North–London Marylebone and the evening return 1U50, the 17.21 London Marylebone–Banbury.

## Class 68 diagrams

Monday 9 January–Sunday 19 May 2023 – note on weekends any engineering blockades mean that all trains shown below will be substituted by Class 168 DMUs.

Class 68 and Mk 3 TSO and Mk 3 TSO and Mk 3 TSO and Mk 3 TSO and Mk 3 TSO and Mk 3a RFM and Mk 3 DVT (note some rakes may be short formed by one Mk 3 TSO vehicle)

**Monday–Friday**
**Diagram 1**
1H12 07.40 Princes Risborough–London Marylebone (arr 08.32)
1R93 12.10 London Marylebone–Birmingham Moor Street (arr 1.56)
1H53 14.55 Birmingham Moor Street–London Marylebone (arr 16.43)
1K52 17.46 London Marylebone–Kidderminster (arr 20.23)

**Diagram 2**
1H17 06.41 Stourbridge Junction–London Marylebone (arr 09.09)
1R91 10.10 London Marylebone–Birmingham Moor Street (arr 11.56)
1H45 12.55 Birmingham Moor Street–London Marylebone (arr 14.53)
1K48 16.46 London Marylebone–Kidderminster (arr 19.23)

**68013, at the time unnamed, pauses at Birmingham Snow Hill on 28 November 2015, with 1K50, the 17.15 London Marylebone–Kidderminster. Steam-era enthusiasts, or even fans of the Western Diesel Hydraulics that used to ply their trade along the line, would struggle to recognise the formerly elegant environs of Snow Hill – now surrounding by tall buildings.**

**Diagram 3**
1H14 06.30 Birmingham Moor Street–London Marylebone (arr 08.36)

**Saturdays**
**Diagram 1**
1H13 07.12 Kidderminster–London Marylebone (arr 09.53)
1R24 11.00 London Marylebone–Birmingham Moor Street (arr 13.06)
1H37 13.37 Birmingham Moor Street–London Marylebone (arr 15.49)
1K48 17.00 London Marylebone–Kidderminster (arr 19.41)

**Diagram 2**
1H11 06.37 Kidderminster–London Marylebone (arr 09.14)
1R30 12.37 London Marylebone–Birmingham Moor Street (arr 14.36)
1H43 15.14 Birmingham Moor Street–London Marylebone (arr 17.12)
1K58 19.37 London Marylebone–Kidderminster (arr 22.09)

**Sundays**
**Diagram 1**
1H25 10.00 Kidderminster–London Marylebone (arr 12.47)
1K48 17.00 London Marylebone–Kidderminster (arr 19.41)

**Diagram 2**
1H27 10.30 Kidderminster–London Marylebone (arr 13.28)
1K58 19.37 London Marylebone–Kidderminster (arr 22.09)

On 20 October 2015, 68008 *Avenger* pauses at Leamington Spa while working 1H62, the 15.55 Birmingham Moor Street–London Marylebone. In Platform 1, a Class 168 is arriving on a Marylebone–Birmingham Snow Hill train.

On 19 March 2015, early in its career on Chiltern services, 68011 stands at London Marylebone with the 19.10 to Kidderminster.

68010 waits in the up sidings at Banbury on the evening of 27 October 2015 with the full rake of Cargo-d Mark 3 slam-door coaches on hire to Chiltern at the time. The diagram for this stock, with a Class 68, was 1H06, the 06.10 Banbury to London Marylebone and return 1U50, 17.21 back to Banbury from Marylebone. Chiltern later bought their own rake of unrefurbished Mark 3s for use on these services (including some previously bought from Cargo-d by Wrexham and Shropshire), but they had to be withdrawn by 1 January 2020.

Chapter 3

# Railtours and Preserved Railway Workings

In 2007, DRS began to expand into passenger services, in association with Stobart Rail, overhauling a rake of seven ex-Virgin Mk 3 coaches for charter and short-term hire. DRS locos and stock were also provided for short-term hire for use on scheduled passenger services, namely the Fife Circle, the Wherry Lines (Norfolk) and around the Cumbrian Coast.

By 2009, DRS was providing standby locos to National Express East Anglia, which included the provision of dragging locos for use during engineering work, or more regular duties including the haulage of summer-dated Liverpool Street–Yarmouth trains over the unelectrified final section from Norwich.

Ad hoc passenger duties included the 'Floodexes' – shuttle trains operated between April 2009 and May 2010 between Maryport and Workington after a road bridge in Workington was washed away by floods (the trains filling the gap and avoiding a lengthy road journey). Locos provided included Classes 37, 47 and 57.

**In the days before 68025 *Superb* plied its trade with TPE, in its new all-over blue colours, the DRS-liveried loco stands at Birmingham International on the evening of 12 December 2017 with a return 'Northern Belle' luxury excursion.**

## Northern Belle

DRS further expanded its passenger services in April 2011 with a five-year contract for provision of locos and crew for the 'Northern Belle' land-cruise train, the *Orient Express of the North*, generally working in top-and-tail mode and replacing the previously used DB Schenker Class 47s. Newly introduced, the Class 68 shared the duties initially with two specially repainted Class 47s, but later the service mostly used dedicated Class 57/3s 57305 and 57312. Class 68s were used in the event of the 57s not being available, or if the timing required 160km/h (100mph) running – often into and out of London termini. Despite some complaints that the 68s caused some jolting due to the blended braking system, the locos proved popular on the trains.

The 'Northern Belle' services took the 68s to new and far-flung locations, including Carmarthen, Fishguard, Penzance, Inverness and Margate, with unusual lines including the Central Wales and Bicester–Claydon–Aylesbury (currently being rebuilt for the East-West Rail Project). Class 68s made their debut on the northern part of the East Coast Main Line on 9 August 2015, when 68008 hauled a 'Northern Belle' working from London King's Cross to Inverness.

In November 2017, the 'Northern Belle' operation was purchased by David Smith of West Coast Railways, together with businessman David Pitts, and from April 2018 traction has been provided by West Coast's Class 57s.

## Passenger services

The first passenger workings for Class 68s took place in Scotland, on additional relief services on 23 September 2014 with 68005 and 68006 working top-and-tail on 1Z25, the 06.23 Glasgow Central–Gleneagles, in connection with the Ryder Cup golf event being held that week. The locos went on to work a number of other services between Perth and Glasgow over the next few days.

Following a successful trial in May 2015, passenger services from Carlisle to Sellafield (mainly for the use of staff at the plant), DRS and Northern signed a contract to provide cover for a DMU shortage along the Cumbrian Coast.

## Galas and railtours

After the introduction of the Class 68s into traffic, enthusiast interest in the new locos was at a very high level, with many requests for use at diesel galas. DRS Class 68 68007 visited the Mid Norfolk Railway on 28 December 2014 during the Christmas Diesel Gala, the first time a Class 68 had visited a preserved railway, with the loco proving very popular and performing impeccably.

The first planned railtour for the new class was booked for 19 July 2014 and Pathfinder Railtour's 'Caterpillar Cat', running from Eastleigh up the Lickey Incline then via Shrewsbury and Chester to Crewe (in association with the DRS Crewe Charity Open Day, held on the same date, where DRS proudly displayed some of its new fleet). This had been booked for 68 haulage, to be run on 19 July 2014, but was replaced by two Class 57s at short notice.

The first railtour duty to be hauled by a Class 68 took place later in the year, on 6 December, when 68014 hauled the 'Yuletide Yorkshire Explorer', running as 1Z68 from Newport to Leeds and 1Z69 return.

# Chapter 4
# East Anglia – The Wherry Lines

The Wherry Lines, from Norwich to Great Yarmouth and Lowestoft, proved to be one of the last bastions for the locomotive-hauled train in recent years, with 'short sets' (three, or even fewer Mk 2s) also being introduced to provide vital additional capacity and as a substitute for DMUs unavailable due to collision damage (due in no small part to level crossing collisions) or wheelflat issues. Greater Anglia needed to run 21 DMU diagrams daily with only 26 sets available; taking into account regular and cyclical heavy maintenance requirements, meant that the loco-hauled sets were essential.

The Wherry Lines (named after the single-masted sailing boats that used to ply the local waters), run from Norwich to Great Yarmouth and Lowestoft. The lines have a strong regional identity, and the local people are proud of their railway. That sense of place and community is shared by the Wherry Lines Community Rail Partnership (CRP) and Greater Anglia, which work closely together to develop the lines.

The routes are generally double track except for the single lines from Brundall to Great Yarmouth via Acle (where trains can pass) and Reedham to Great Yarmouth via Berney Arms. They have a loading gauge of W8, except between Lowestoft and Oulton Broad North Junction where it is W6.

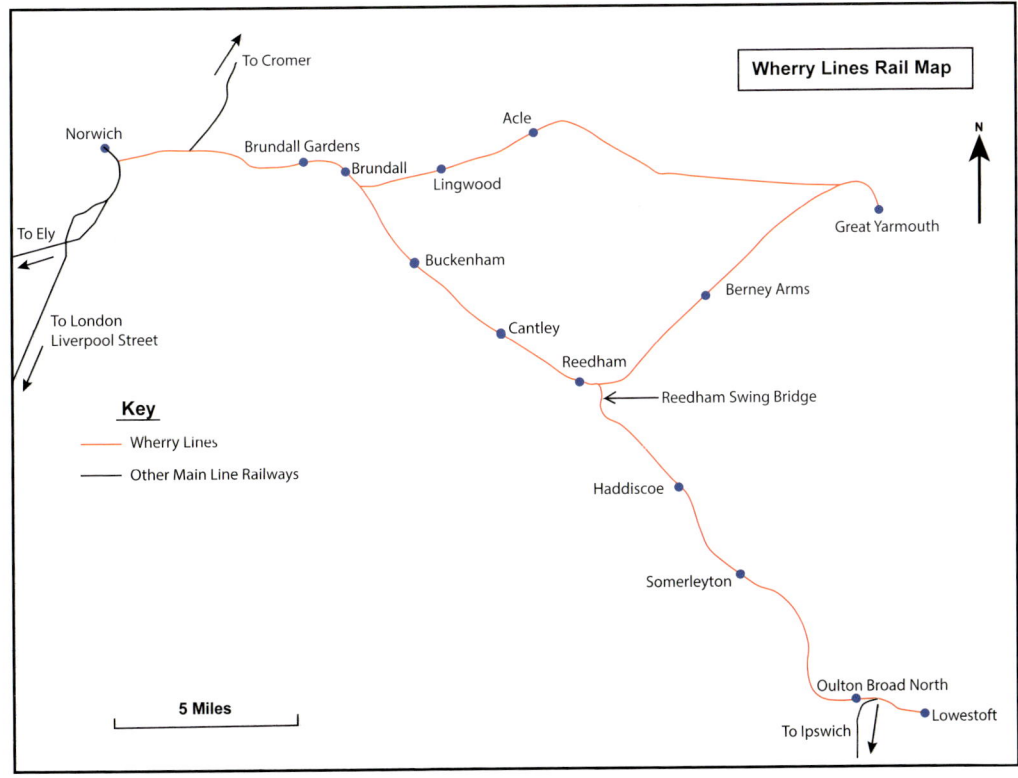

Line speed on the routes varies from 64–96km/h (40–60mph) with a number of 32km/h (20mph) restrictions including Reedham Swing Bridge, Reedham Junction, and a fragile bridge just to the west of Brundall Gardens. There is also a 48km/h (30mph) restriction over Somerleyton Swing Bridge and 24–40km/h (15–25mph) over Brundall Junction. The only significant gradient on the route is Brundall Bank.

The short, low platform at Berney Arms prevents locos and stock calling there, though this caused few difficulties as the station is very sparsely used.

When regular loco-hauled services in the area ended in 1984, followed by only summer-dated hauled services to Yarmouth, no one imagined that more than 30 years later enthusiasts would be able to enjoy 13 diesel-hauled services per day to and from Norwich (and 25 or 29 during the period when Class 68s were covering for a damaged Class 170 from July 2016 to September 2017).

The region saw the last daily passenger diagram for Class 47s operated from April 2004 – a London to Norwich train operated as a through service to Yarmouth as a franchise agreement commitment. Poor passenger numbers saw this service replaced by a Class 170 from September 2005.

In 2003–2005, Cotswold Rail Class 47s were used on ad hoc short-set operations, but improved DMU availability saw these workings virtually disappear until DRS took over the provisions of Class 47s to the operators (by then known as National Express East Anglia (NXEA)) for ad hoc duties, including occasional Wherry Lines substitutions and additional services for the annual Lowestoft airshows, from June 2009.

From 2005, following reliability issues with the Cotswold Rail Class 47 standby locos, DRS took over the contract to supply three Class 47s, the first hire deal for DRS with a train operating company (TOC). Some through services also involved the Class 90 being dragged through to Yarmouth with maximum speed of 80km/h (50mph) due to gauging issues (concerns that the pantograph may strike low bridges).

**On 13 July 2016, 68016** *Fearless* **rests at Norwich after arrival on 2P35, the 18.47 Great Yarmouth–Norwich via Reedham. 68019** *Brutus* **is at the front of the train, ready to return the service as 2P40, the 20.38 Norwich–Great Yarmouth via Acle.**

On 28 July 2016, 68019 waits in the Up Sidings at Norwich with an East Anglian 'short set', with 68016 *Fearless* at the rear.

68017 *Hornet* waits at Great Yarmouth with 68005 *Defiant* on the rear, on 17 January 2017, on 2P34, the 18.06 from Norwich.

On 17 April 2017, 68019 *Brutus* arrives at Oulton Broad North with 2J73, the 10.57 Lowestoft–Norwich service. 68018 *Vigilant* was the loco at the rear. The impressive semaphore signals along the Wherry Lines were all removed in February 2020.

From 2010, with a need to refurbish a number of DMUs and growing passenger demand, top-and-tail Class 47s began to see more regular use with a fixed Monday to Friday diagram introduced. From 2011 onwards, with a short gap in 2012, a short set of loco-hauled stock saw regular use on Wherry Lines trains.

By 2010, a huge growth in passenger traffic had left the operator, by now National Express, very short of units and Class 47s returned to the area, paired with hauled stock. Top-and-tail DRS Class 47s began to be used, hauling NXEA Mk 3s, the trigger being the withdrawal for repairs of a Class 156, 156417, which had struck a lorry on a level crossing on the Sudbury Branch.

In 2014, Greater Anglia negotiated a deal to retain locomotive haulage, initially using Class 47s hired from DRS. However, with the increasing unreliability of the 47s, the freight company, with the support of GA, immediately began plans to replace the 47s with 37/4s. The timing of the changeover was determined by the availability of the Class 37s and crew training requirements at GA, so the transition took place on 16 June 2015, with 37405 and 37425 starting their duties, and the 37s remaining in service on these trains for several years.

A nationwide shortage of DMUs had contributed to the need to hire the loco-hauled sets with the Anglian operators only able to secure short-term hire of ATW 150/2s and LM 153s.

Nevertheless, increased demand for DMUs meant that extra capacity was needed, and the Wherry Lines, with their longer runs, higher speeds, higher loadings and fewer stops, are the most suitable for locos and stock. They also have self-contained diagrams based out of Norwich, enabling a more efficient and resilient deployment of trains and crew.

Ad hoc arrangements with DRS, evolved into regular short-term hire from 2012/13, with a more formal longer-term leasing arrangement for 47s agreed before Abellio's second franchise (July 2014 to October 2016) began. With concerns about 47 reliability and availability, and the opportunity for introduction of DRS's refurbished 37 fleet, GA changed its traction requirements to 37s as soon as sufficient DRS examples became available.

Class 37 driver-training began in March 2015 (comprising a two-day conversion course) with the locos taking over in traffic from June. The Class 37s were through-wired, enabling full push-pull operation, though this was often disabled, with a single 37 still generally able to keep DMU timings.

Greater Anglia had originally considered the use of Driving Brake Standard Opens (DBSO) with single 37s (as used on the Cumbrian Coast) but opted for the greater inbuilt reliability of top-and-tail working. Northern had paid for the second Class 37 used in Anglia until the Abellio-owned Northern franchise ended in March 2016.

The 37s, from the XHAC Pool, were serviced at Crown Point on Sundays, with the work contracted out to Arlington Fleet Services of Eastleigh. More extensive exams were carried out at Crewe Gresty Lane with locos swapped every few weeks. The DRS 37/4s used on the Cumbrian Coast belonged to a separate pool, XHCC, although XHAC 37425 was seen on hire for Cumbrian Coast duties for some of the last year.

**On 16 August 2017, 68005, with 68028 on the rear, arrives at Norwich on 2J37, the 10.57 Lowestoft–Norwich.**

On 28 December 2016, a number of cancellations saw 68025 and 68001 parked with the three-coach short set of Mk 2s, in the frosty sidings at Norwich, awaiting their next turn of duty on the Wherry Lines. On the following day, the two locomotives were back in action, working 2J70, the 10.05 to Lowestoft.

The iconic swing bridge at Reedham is crossed by 68005 *Defiant*, with 68017 on the rear, on 17 January 2017, on 2J73, the 10.57 Lowestoft–Norwich service.

**68017 *Hornet* pauses at the quaint country station at Brundall on the line from Norwich to the branches at Lowestoft and Great Yarmouth. 68005 *Hornet* was dead on the rear of the train.**

Reliability and availability issues periodically affected the 37-hauled services in East Anglia (and the Mk 2 carriages have had some air-conditioning and toilet issues), but the 37s proved to be significantly more reliable than the 47s they replaced. In order to further increase reliability with the short sets, DRS was asked to provide Class 68s to replace some of the Class 37s in use.

In preparation for the use of 68s on Lowestoft and Great Yarmouth services, 68016 *Fearless* and 68023 *Achilles* were used in 2016 empty circular training runs, operating as 5Z60, 11.02 Norwich–Norwich.

The Class 68-hauled short set, hired from Riviera Trains via DRS, was brought into use in 2016 following a collision between 170204 and a tractor on Hockham Road level crossing, near Thetford, on 10 April 2016, on the 12.03 Norwich–Cambridge service. Class 230 'D-Train' units were considered for short-term hire, but were ruled out as the training and route clearance involved meant it would have taken too long to mobilise them and at that stage the 230s hadn't yet been used in public service.

The extent of the repair needed for the Class 170 meant that what was originally seen as a six to nine-month operation became a 12-month period, which was then extended to September 2017 to facilitate the fitting of wheel-slip protection equipment to GA's Class 156s, in an innovative project that has markedly improved DMU performance in the challenging autumn period.

DRS began driver training for Class 68s on 2 July 2016 with 68016 and 68023. The locos operated in top-and-tail mode (with only the leading locomotive powering and one loco providing ETH usually the one at the Norwich end of the rake). The stock was comprised of three Mk 2F carriages hired from Riviera Trains comprising Standard Opens (TSOs) 5921/950 and Brake Standard Open (BSO) 9520, previously based at Burton. The hire of the Class 68s and stock was funded via Network Rail as part of the insurance claim from the level-crossing collision. Longer-term hire was ruled out due to the higher leasing costs for the 68s compared to the 37s.

The 68s were driven by DRS crews, originally outbased at Stowmarket. DRS drivers (three per day) were used due to the warranty deal on the fleet with Vossloh. After some additional crew training, route learning and route clearance the 68s began service on 11 July 2016. The set was classified as NC68 for diagramming purposes, complementing NC37, the 37-hauled set. The 68s were serviced in a 12-hour window on Crown Point on Saturdays.

68025 *Superb* passes Haddiscoe Bridge on the rear of train 2J73, the 10.57 Lowestoft–Norwich on the 3 January 2017. Sister loco 68005 *Defiant* was hauling the service. While Haddiscoe village is almost two miles away, the village of St Olaves is just the other side of the River Waveney, shown on the photo, with a fishing vessel having ventured in land, away from the rest of the Lowestoft fleet.

On 17 April 2017, 68019 *Brutus* departs from Oulton Broad North with 2J70, the 10.05 Norwich–Lowestoft service. 68018 *Vigilant* was the loco at the front.

## Anglian Class 68 diagrams
**Monday to Friday, NC68, 11 July 2016–8 September 2017**
2P06 06.52 Norwich–Great Yarmouth (via Acle) (arr 07.26)
2P07 07.30 Great Yarmouth–Norwich (via Acle) (arr 08.05)
2P10 08.09 Norwich–Great Yarmouth (via Acle) (arr 08.42)
2P11 08.46 Great Yarmouth–Norwich (via Acle) (arr 09.19)
2J70 10.05 Norwich–Lowestoft (Arrive 10.52)
2J73 10.57 Lowestoft–Norwich (Arrive 11.35)
2P28 16.38 Norwich–Great Yarmouth (via Acle) (arr 17.13)
2P29 17.17 Great Yarmouth–Norwich (via Acle) (arr 17.55)
2P34 18.04 Norwich–Great Yarmouth (via Acle) (arr 18.41)
2P35 18.47 Great Yarmouth–Norwich (via Reedham) (arr 19.25)
2P40 20.38 Norwich–Great Yarmouth (via Acle) (arr 21.13)
2P41 21.17 Great Yarmouth–Norwich (via Acle) (arr 21.52)
2J94 22.05 Norwich–Lowestoft (arr 22.52)

## ECS to Norwich Crown Point
At times of unit shortage, the Class 68 set also additionally worked the following trains:
2J74 12.05 Norwich–Lowestoft (arr 12.50)
2J77 12.57 Lowestoft–Norwich (arr 11.35)
2J78 14.05 Norwich–Lowestoft (arr 14.50)
2J81 14.57 Lowestoft–Norwich (arr 15.33)

Class 68s used on the Wherry Lines passenger services between July 2016 and September 2017 were 68001–68005, 68009, 68016–68019, 68021–68025, 68027 and 68028, though in the case of 68027 it only worked one morning before failing, and 68009 only covered a few services.

**On 28 December 2016, 68025** *Superb* **stands at Norwich with fellow Class 68 68005** *Defiant* **on the rear, ticking over.**

68016 *Fearless* arrives at Norwich on 10 August 2016, with 68019 *Brutus* on the rear, working 2J73, the 10.57 Lowestoft–Norwich, Greater Anglia service.

Friday 8 September 2017 proved to be the last regular day for timetabled Class 68 operations over the Wherry Lines, with 68001 and 68028 appearing, together with around 100 Class 68 fans from all over the country, to pay their respects. Three days later, the three Mk 2 coaches (5961, 6024 and 9504) were moved away as 5Z29, the 08.13 Norwich–Burton, hauled by 57002 and 68028.

On Saturday 16 September, GA marked the end of the diesel loco-hauled era with a special charity trip using an intercity Mk 3 set on the same itinerary as the Class 37 charity trip in April 2016. 68001 and 68034 top-and-tailed the trip from Norwich–Ely–Norwich–London Liverpool Street–Norwich. The trip raised £12,500 for East Anglia Children's Hospices.

Class 68s returned to the Wherry Lines over the weekend of the 16 and 17 June 2018 to operate a number of additional non-stop workings top-and-tail on full length rakes of GA Mk 3s with 68001, 68002, 68004 and 68018 running non-stop shuttles between Norwich and Great Yarmouth to ferry visitors to and from the seaside town for an airshow event being held there.

# Chapter 5
# Cumbrian Coast

Prior to recent DRS services, diesel-hauled trains on the Cumbrian Coast Line had been something of a rarity, except for some excursion and railtour traffic, with Maryport being a common starting point for British Rail Adex excursions, often to Aberystwyth. These services ran until the 1980s and were usually powered by Class 25s or Class 40s. Class 108 DMUs were the mainstay of regular timetabled passenger services on the line following the end of steam. Introduced in 1960 and allocated to Carlisle Kingmoor shed until its closure in 1988, the 108 DMUs were transferred to Heaton after that date and were replaced by Class 153s in November 1991.

Before the introduction of regular hauled services by DRS in 2015, locomotive haulage around the coast was a rarity, comprising occasional charter and excursion traffic (mostly to and from Maryport and Barrow) and some Class 25s, 40s and 47s, and less commonly Class 26s, dragging failed Class 108 DMUs, though the 108s were very reliable units and DMU drags were relatively rare. Up until the end of the Class 25 fleet in 1987, the Type 2s were the most common rescue loco for Cumbrian Coast Line DMUs with the Class 47s taking over the occasional drag till the introduction of the Class 153s, bringing to an end more than 30 years of locomotive rescue duties on the route.

Gauging issues, a consequence of the minimal loading gauge inherited from the original Maryport and Carlisle Railway, meant that stock used on the line, including the Class 108 DMUs, had been fitted with bars on the drop light windows to prevent window-hanging passengers suffering head injuries. Several bridges in particular have very minimal clearance on the section between Maryport and Carlisle. The regular loco-hauled Mk 2 stock used on the line by DRS/Northern is similarly equipped while any

68003 *Astute* nears Netherton on 12 July 2018 on 2C47, the 17.31 Barrow-in-Furness–Carlisle service, with the famed Sellafield nuclear reprocessing plant in the background.

On Wednesday 12 September 2018, Class 68033, with 68005 *Defiant* leading, leaves St Bees with 2C59, the 14.52 Barrow–Carlisle service.

charter traffic must be stewarded between Maryport and Carlisle to prevent passengers placing their heads out of windows.

Some charter operators insist that all passengers remain seated over this section and a steam ban (due to gauging issues) was in place in the early years of preserved mainline steam between Maryport and Carlisle. Steam tours over the route are now very popular and despite pathing restrictions, Network Rail has managed to fit a steam path in the timetable for Saturdays – a 14.06 departure from Carlisle, allowing for a water stop at Sellafield.

Following severe flooding in Cumbria in 2009, and the washing away of the main through road bridge in Workington, an hourly loco-hauled service was introduced between Maryport and Workington, also calling at a new temporary station – Workington North, to avoid a long road journey for locals and visitors. The extras, referred to by enthusiasts and some staff as the Floodexes, ran from 27 November to December 2009 and locomotives featured included 37423 and 47832, 37610, 47501, 57007 and 57008 with three DRS Mk 3s and an Mk 2 BSO on hire from West Coast Railway Company (WCRC).

DRS, buoyed by the success of the Floodexes, introduced a trial service on 9 January 2012, between Carlisle and Sellafield, catering for workers at the plant, using a Class 37 and four Mk 2 coaches. The stock for the trial service had been bought by DRS and overhauled at Eastleigh after use in East Anglia. The trial was deemed a success and rumours persisted that the company would begin regular use of the locos and stock, but it was to be almost three years before the company restored regular loco-hauled services over the route. The trial service allowed an arrival in Sellafield from Carlisle at 07.55, compared to the previous earliest arrival of 10:11. Management at the Sellafield plant was keen to discourage car use, with roads in the area becoming increasingly congested with worker commuter traffic and Lake District tourists. Around 550 workers use rail to travel to the Sellafield plant every day, reducing pressure on the local road network.

The unlikely introduction of Class 37s on regular, timetabled, loco-hauled services around the Cumbrian Coast Line from 2015 was the result of a complex series of rolling stock transfers. As TPE

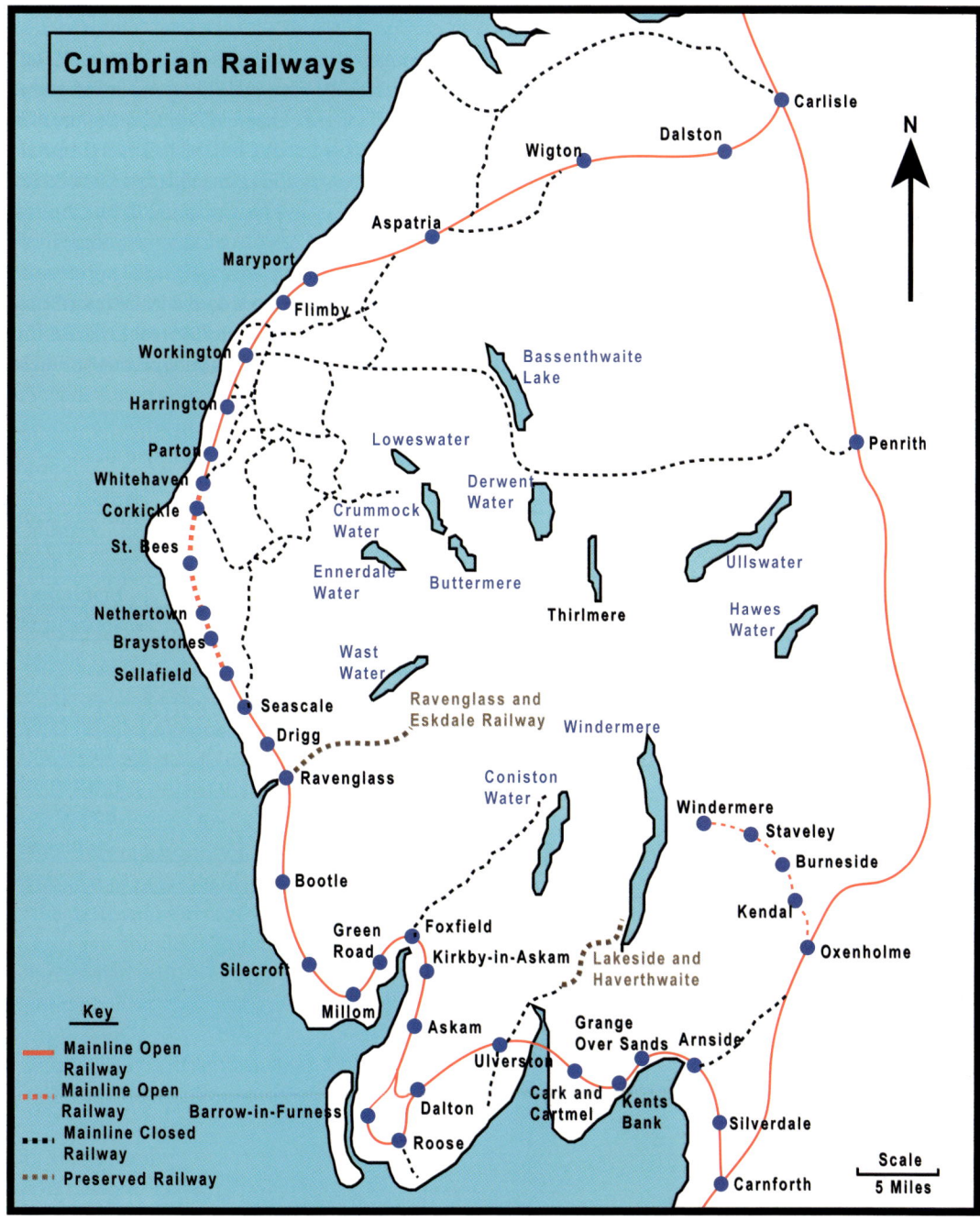

neared the end of its franchise, the lease on its small fleet of Class 170s expired. The ROSCO was unwilling to extend the lease, being offered a better deal by Chiltern, which could hire them for a longer period. The subsequent stock shortage saw responsibility for operations shuffled between TPE and Northern, with Northern hiring the DRS locos and stock to make up for the shortfall of Class 156s (used to provide rolling stock for the yet-to-be-electrified Manchester–Blackpool line.

DRS, with Department for Transport (DfT) backing and funding, signed a two-year contract with Northern in 2015, with an option for a two-year extension, for the provision of locos and stock. The stock carries DfT branding to highlight the financial support provided by the government body.

Regular locomotive-hauled passenger services, to increase capacity and release DMUs for use elsewhere on the Northern network, recommenced over the route from the timetable change in May 2015. Initially, one of the sets ran through to Preston Mondays to Fridays, and through to Lancaster on Saturday. Northern hired two sets of locomotives and coaches, initially until 6 January 2019. The first day of regular loco-hauled operations (on 19 May 2015) saw 37423 and 37609 working top-and-tail on one set of stock (comprised of 9507, 6122, 5810 and 6173) with 37419 and 37605 (and 9527, 5995, 5971 and 6001) on the other set. The regular XHCC pool of DRS Class 37/4s for Cumbrian services comprises 37401–403, 424 and 425.

Before Driving Brake Standard Opens (DBSO) became available, the services were operated by 37s in top-and-tail with several exotic 'no-heat' locos making an appearance, as detailed below. DBSO 9705 began crew training in July 2015 with 37401 and 37604. A DBSO replaced the Class 37 on one of the sets from 27 July 2015, with the other replaced a few weeks later. The DBSOs had been originally converted for use on Class 47/7 powered Edinburgh–Glasgow shuttles in 1979.

The loco-hauled sets were not used on Sundays with Northern able to provide sufficient DMUs for the recently reintroduced service over the route on those days.

| Locos and stock used on Cumbrian Coast loco-hauled services (2015–18) |
|---|
| **Class 37/0** |
| 37218, 37259 |
| **Class 37/4** |
| 37401, 37402, 37403, 37405, 37409, 37419, 37422, 37423, 37424, 37425, |
| **Class 37/6** |
| 37602, 37603, 37604, 37605, 37606, 37608, 37609, 37610, 37611, 37612, 37688, |
| **Class 37/7** |
| 37716 |
| **Class 57/3** |
| 57302, 57308 |
| **Class 68** |
| 68003, 68004, 68005, 68016, 68017, 68018, 68022, 68025 |
| **Mk 2 Coaching Stock** |
| **Mk 2D** |
| **BFK** 17159 |
| **Mk 2E** |
| **TSOs** 5787, 5810 |
| **BSOs** 9506, 9507, 9527 |
| **Mk 2F** |
| **TSOs** 5919, 5971, 5995, 6001, 6008, 6046, 6064, 6117, 6122, 6173 |
| **DBSOs** 9704, 9705, 9707, 9709, 9710 |

| Locos and stock used on Cumbrian Coast loco-hauled services (2015–18) |
|---|
| **Remarks** |
| Mk 2D and E coaches 9506, 9507, 9527 and 17159 – short-term hires from Riviera |
| Mk 2F TSOs are DRS-liveried and fitted with Selective Door Opening (SDO), Window Bars and Controlled Emission Toilets (CET) |
| 37602 worked 15/03/16 Sellafield–Carlisle with 37402 on rear |
| 37608 worked 17.37 Carlisle–Barrow only, on 2 December 2015 |
| 37610 worked 31 July 2015 only |
| 37716 worked 12 February 2016 and 4 May 2016 |
| 57302 rescued 37402 on 17.30 Barrow–Carlisle from Wigton on 14 May 2015 |
| 57308 rescued 37424 from Parton N Jn to Workington (caped) 17 April 2018 |
| 68022 rescued 37403 on 08.45 Barrow–Carlisle from Aspatria 24 July 2017 |
| 68025 and 68016 dragged 37401 back into Ulverston on 28 February 2018 |

Concerns about the reliability of the Class 37/4s and DBSOs used on Cumbrian services were discussed at the end of 2017. DRS was approached to provide Class 68s in top-and-tail mode for the route.

DRS began training staff with Class 68s and loco-hauled stock on 8 January 2018 with its own set of three Mk 2s top-and-tailed by 68029 and 68003, running as 5Z57, the 07.50 Carlisle Kingmoor–Carnforth and 5Z58, 12.40 return with the intention of replacing one of the Northern-operated Class 37 sets on Cumbrian Coast diagrams in the spring.

From 12 March 2018, one of the hauled sets was worked by top-and-tail Class 68s (with the trailing Class 68 not providing traction power), and with the other set in use daily remaining Class 37-powered, together with a DBSO. Class 68 haulage began initially using 68017 and 68018, and from that date the pairs comprised 68004 and 68017, 68004 and 68003, 68017 and 68003, and 68005 and 68033.

**68033 waits at Barrow-in-Furness on 12 September 2018, on 2C40, the 17.45 from Carlisle. 68005 *Defiant*, on the rear, would drag the set into the carriage sidings to await their next turn of duty.**

On 20 April 2018, 68004 *Rapid* arrives at Barrow from the sidings, with empty stock, to form train 2C59, the 14.52 Barrow-in-Furness–Carlisle. 68017 *Hornet* would haul the train forward to Carlisle.

68018 *Vigilant* is hauled out of Dalston by train loco 68017 Hornet, which is on the front, on Wednesday 28 March 2018, on 2C45, the 09.18 Barrow-in-Furness–Carlisle.

From the introduction of Class 68s in March 2018, the two diagrams on the coast consisted of one rake of four coaches, with a DBSO and 37/4, and another shorter rake with top-and-tail 68s and three coaches (shorter due to restricted platform lengths and the addition of an extra loco).

| Set consists on Cumbrian loco-hauled trains (early 2018) | | | | | | |
|---|---|---|---|---|---|---|
| KM03 | 37/4 | 6008 | 6046 | 5971 | 9705 (DBSO) | |
| KM04 | 37/4 | 5919 | 6064 | 6122 | 9710 (DBSO) | |
| KM05 | 68 | 5995 | 6173 | 9709 | 68 | |
| KM06 | 68 | 6001 | 9506 | 9707 | 68 | |

Crewing arrangements for the loco-hauled services on the Cumbrian were complicated and difficult at times, with DRS often having its own driver and guard on the train with a Northern/Northern Rail conductor selling tickets and Northern drivers also on hand. Train crew were based at Barrow-in-Furness and Workington for coast passenger services.

Class 37s were generally restricted to a minimum of four coaches on the loco-hauled trains, to allow sufficient brake force to run at line speed, though on occasions the sets were run as load 3. Class 68s, with their more advanced braking systems, were allowed fewer coaches (a maximum of three) – with platform lengths and the extra loco on the rear of the 68-hauled trains also being a factor.

The use of Class 68s on Cumbrian services ended on Saturday 15 September 2018, with 68033 and 68005 *Defiant* working the usual top-and-tail Saturday Class 68 diagram, ending at Carlisle at 18.14 then working the stock empty back to Carlisle Kingmoor.

The last day of DRS's loco-hauled services on the Cumbrian Coast was 28 December 2018 with 37425 *Sir Robert McAlpine* and 37588 *Avro Vulcan XH558* featuring.

## Cumbrian Coast locomotive-hauled diagrams (valid May to September 2018)
### Northern–Cumbrian Coast (operated by DRS)
**Monday–Friday**
**Diagram 1**
**Class 37 TThO, Class 68 MWFO**
5C40 05.54 ECS Kingmoor Sdgs–Carlisle (arr 06.04)
2C40 06.16 Carlisle–Barrow (arr 08.54)
2C45 09.18 Barrow–Carlisle (arr 11.57)
2C52 12.08 Carlisle–Barrow (arr 14.41)
2C59 14.52 Barrow–Carlisle (arr 17.30)
2C40 17.45 Carlisle–Barrow (arr 20.37)
5C40 20.45 ECS Barrow–Barrow CS

**Diagram 2**
**Class 37 MWFO, Class 68 TThO**
5C35 05.37 ECS Barrow CS–Barrow (arr 05.40)
2C35 05.50 Barrow–Carlisle (arr 08.42)
2C46 09.03 Carlisle–Barrow (arr 11.45)
5C46 11.51 ECS Barrow–Barrow CS (arr 11.54)
5C33 15.17 ECS Barrow CS–Barrow (arr 15.20)
2C33 15.31 Barrow–Carlisle (arr 18.11)
5C33 18.21 ECS Carlisle–Kingmoor (arr 18.33)

**Saturdays**
**Diagram 1**
**Class 37-hauled**
5C35 05.37 ECS Barrow CS–Barrow (arr 05.40)
2C35 05.50 Barrow–Carlisle (arr 08.42)
2C46 08.51 Carlisle–Barrow (arr 11.41)
5C46 11.51 ECS Barrow–Barrow CS (arr 11.54)
5C33 15.17 ECS Barrow CS–Barrow (arr 15.20)
2C33 15.31 Barrow–Carlisle (arr 18.14)
5C33 18.21 ECS Carlisle–Kingmoor (arr 18.33)

**Diagram 2**
**Class 68-hauled**
5C40 05.54 ECS Kingmoor Sdgs–Carlisle (arr 06:04)
2C40 06.16 Carlisle–Barrow (arr 08.54)
2C45, 09.02 Barrow–Carlisle (arr 11.51)
2C52 12.08 Carlisle–Barrow (arr 14.41)
2C59 14.52 Barrow–Carlisle (arr 17.30)
2C40 17.45 Carlisle–Barrow (arr 20.37)
5C40 20.45 ECS Barrow–Barrow CS

*Left*: 68018 *Vigilant* arrives into Dalston with trailing loco 68017 *Hornet* on the rear, on Wednesday 28 March 2018, on 2C52, the 12.08 Carlisle–Barrow-in-Furness.

*Below*: 68018 *Vigilant* is hauled out of Barrow by train loco 68017 *Hornet*, on the front, on 14 March 2018, after arrival on 2C14, the 10.04 from Preston.

# Chapter 6
# Fife Circle

The Fife Circle, the local rail service for the Kingdom of Fife, north of Edinburgh, was operated by Abellio Scotrail (wholly owned by the Dutch national rail operator Nederlandse Spoorwegen, itself owned by the Dutch government) until Friday 1 April 2022, when it was transferred into public ownership. Under Abellio, the franchise operator used loco-hauled services on some of its commuter services around the Fife Circle, initially with Class 67s, then later with Class 68s.

Services link the towns of South Fife with Edinburgh via the Forth Rail Bridge with trains travelling north along the East Coast and the coastal stations along the Firth of Forth. Starting from Edinburgh Waverley, Fife Circle services travel north along the East Coast Main Line to Inverkeithing (for clockwise services) or Thornton West and South Junctions, (7km/4½ miles north of Kirkcaldy) in the case of anti-clockwise services, before passing through the former Fife Coalfield area.

The train service is primarily composed of two main routes, Edinburgh to Kirkcaldy and Edinburgh to Cowdenbeath (and onwards to Cardenden). Before re-opening in 1989, the anti-clockwise line onwards from

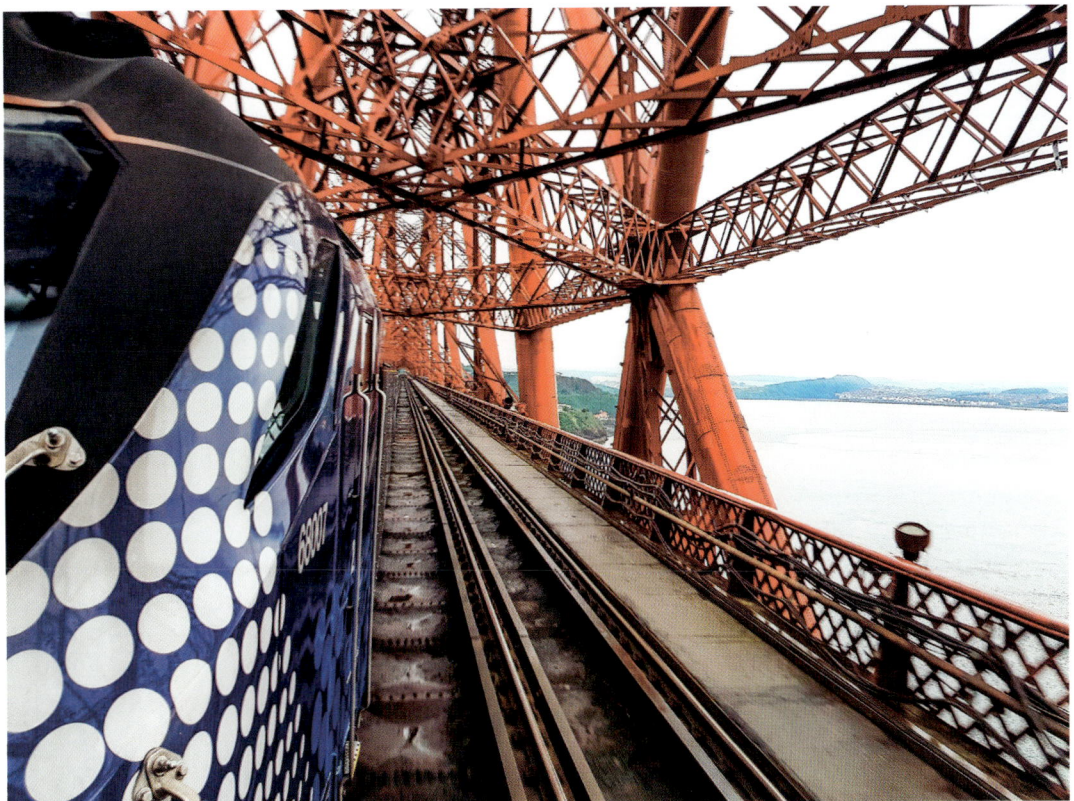

A sight and sound that most of us, if any, are unlikely to ever again experience, the front coach of a loco-hauled service train, crossing the Forth Bridge, with the vestibule window down, enjoying the sights, the sounds and the smells of a Class 68 above the Firth of Forth, deep below. 68007 rumbles across the iconic bridge on 22 January working 2G13, the 17.08 Edinburgh–Glenrothes with Thornton.

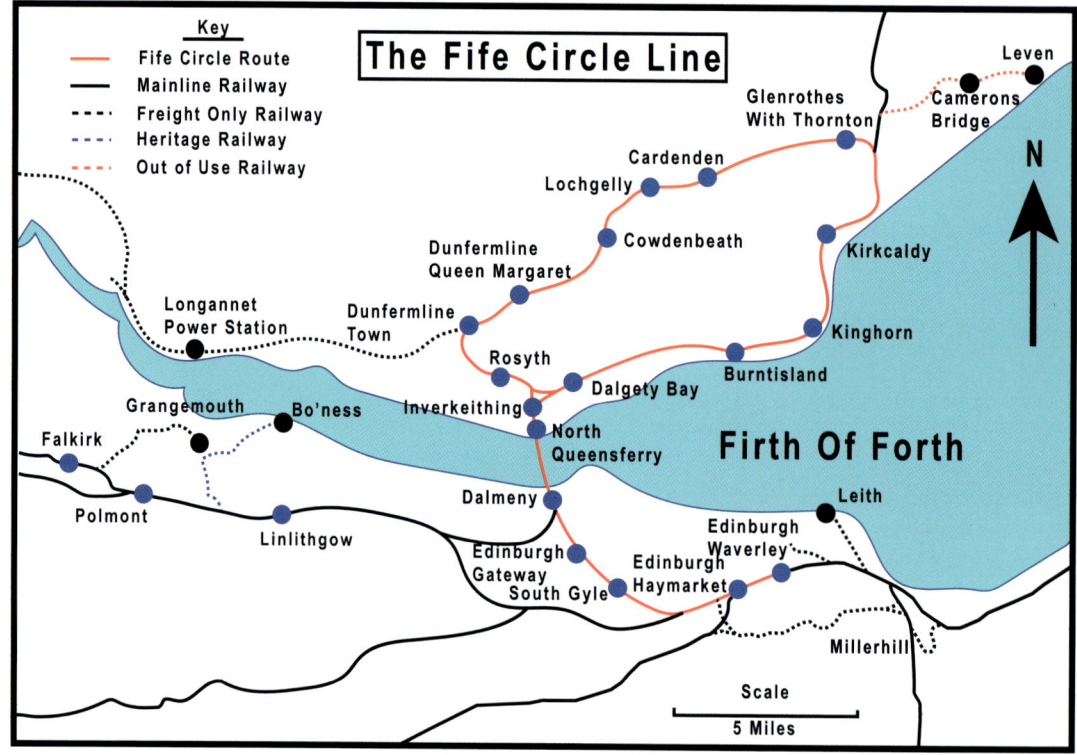

Kirkcaldy to Cardenden via Thornton South and West Junctions was freight only (being closed to passengers in 1969). In the opposite (clockwise) direction, trains run mainly to Cowdenbeath with a few peak services continuing to Cardenden. In 1992, BR opened a new station at Glenrothes and Thornton, followed later by Dalgety Bay in 1998 and Dunfermline Queen Margaret (serving the eponymous adjacent hospital) in 2000. Services now also call at Edinburgh Gateway (for Edinburgh Airport), which was opened in 2016.

With an increase in road traffic and congestion in Edinburgh, the Fife Line saw buoyant growth in passenger numbers. The Fife Circle became one of the busiest routes in Scotland and a priority for ScotRail's investment in rolling stock. Morning and evening peak services could be notoriously overcrowded, and the use of loco-hauled coaching stock has provided much needed additional capacity on these key commuter services.

Following the reopening of the Stirling to Alloa Line in May 2008, capacity over the Forth Bridge was freed up – after some freight was moved on to the new route. As far back as May 2008, First ScotRail had announced its intention to use locomotive-hauled stock and diesel locos to ease overcrowding on the increasingly busy peak hour Fife Circle trains into and out of Edinburgh Waverley. The company initially planned to introduce two extra peak hours loco-hauled services from May 2009.

Despite worries that using slam-door stock may extend journey times, the company tendered for a loco and six hauled coaches to provide one peak-hour morning and evening service around the Fife Circle route from May 2009 through to December 2010. At the time, it was thought that electrification of the Airdrie to Bathgate route would free up additional DMUs to operate on the Fife Line and the loco-hauled service would only be a short-term stopgap.

On 20 February 2015, 68004 was used to haul six Mk 2 coaches (3325, 3333, 3344, 3345, 3390 and 9527), on 5Z68, a 13.49 Crewe high speed to Carlisle Kingmoor empty stock move. The rake of coaches

On 16 December 2015, Scotrail-liveried 68007 *Valiant* arrives at Edinburgh Haymarket working 2G13, the 17.08 Edinburgh–Glenrothes with Thornton.

On 16 December 2015, 68006 *Daring* pauses at Inverkeithing working 2G13, the 17.08 Edinburgh–Glenrothes with Thornton. This loco was renamed *Pride of the North* on 12 November 2021, and has been re-liveried by Nuclear Transport Solutions, the new overseeing body for DRS, in recognition of DRS's work in Scotland and the North of England as part of the COP 26 event, and the trial of hydro-treated vegetable oil (HVO) as an alternative to diesel fuel.

was for use on route-learning from Motherwell around the Fife Circle the following week in preparation for DRS taking over the loco-hauled diagrams from DBS Class 67s from 1 April (coinciding with the new Abellio franchise).

Regular loco-hauled services on the Fife Circle line began on 14 December 2008 with Class 67s hired in from English, Welsh & Scottish Railway (EWS). The company fitted a number of its Class 67 fleet with cast steel brakes and radio electronic token block (RETB) for use on the West Highland Sleeper services and these locos, generally restricted to Scotland, featured highly on the Fife trains. Despite this, all of the Class 67 fleet worked Fife Circle-hauled services at some stage, other than some of the Chiltern-dedicated locos – 67010, 67012, 67013 and 67014.

ScotRail began regular running of the two peak-time loco-hauled services coinciding with the timetable change, comprising a full circuit in the morning and another in the evening. The trains were intended to run until December 2010, when electrification of the Airdrie to Bathgate Line was expected to free up available DMUs to replace the Class 67s and stock, though delays in electrification thwarted this plan.

From May 2011, the diagrams changed to a half circle in the morning and a full circle in the evening. Due to continuing capacity and DMU availability issues, the use of loco-hauled sets has expanded over the years. ScotRail announced, on 26 September 2011, that it would introduce a second hauled set on the Fife Circle to cover for DMU 170393, which had been damaged in the 27 July derailment at Edinburgh Princes Street Gardens.

The overall costs of the locomotive-hauled operations were revealed when the Official Journal of the European Union (OJEU) announced in June 2011 that ScotRail had awarded an extension of the contract for the supply of loco-hauled passenger services on the Fife Circle, worth £3.5m. The contract was for provision of a driver, loco and stock (specified as either air-con Mk 2 or Mk 3). The supplier was to be responsible for maintenance and servicing of the rolling stock, including fuelling of the loco, with the exception of internal cleaning and watering, which was to be carried out by ScotRail.

The end of the First ScotRail franchise, and the takeover by Abellio ScotRail in 2015, saw the contract for provision of locos and stock pass to DRS. On 20 February 2015, 68004 ran from Crewe to Carlisle Kingmoor with five Riviera Trains coaches, en route to DRS Motherwell to begin crew training for the Fife services. The lack of available 37s, and their lower power for some strict point-to-point timings, meant that 68s were the chosen power for the new duties. In preparation, DRS began a programme of crew training in March 2015 using a number of locos, though mainly 68004 and 68009, on empty coaching runs between either Motherwell and Mossend, Carlisle Kingmoor, Carnforth or Preston.

Class 68s took over the Fife Circle peak hours loco-hauled commuter services from the 1 April 2015. Two Class 68s were allocated for the new Fife duties, 68006 *Daring* and 68007 *Valiant*, and were repainted into a ScotRail variant of the standard Class 68 DRS livery with TOC branding and cab surround white dot patterns. On the first working day, Scotrail (Saltire) liveried 68006 had the honour of working the first service in the morning, the 07:35 Cardenden–Edinburgh, together with rebranded Scotrail Mk 2 stock. A second 68-hauled diagram started a few weeks later on the Fife Circle.

In association with Fife Circle workings, Class 68s had made their passenger debut in Scotland on additional Ryder Cup relief trains, with 68006 (with 68005 on the rear) and eight Mk 2 coaches forming an additional 1Z25, the 06.23 Glasgow Central to Gleneagles on Tuesday 23 September 2015. The locos returned on 1Z26, the 18.28 Gleneagles to Glasgow Central.

A wide range of Class 68s worked services on the Fife Circle, covering for the usual dedicated locos: 68006 and 68007. These included 68001–68008, 68016–68025, 68030, 68032 and 68033. The use of 68008 was particularly unusual, this being one of the locos allocated to Chiltern Trains as standby for 68010–68015.

**The first day of Class 68s on revenue-earning passenger services was 23 September 2014. Here 68005** *Defiant* **stands in Dundee West Yard before running empties to Gleneagles to form 1Z26, the 18.28 Gleneagles–Glasgow Central 'Ryder Cup' Golfex, hired in on behalf of ScotRail. Sister 68006** *Daring* **(still in DRS Compass livery, and at this stage on the rear of the train, had earlier in the day worked the first Class 68 passenger service – 1Z25, the 06.23 Glasgow Central–Gleneagles). The locomotives and refurbished Mk 2 stock clearly made an impression with Transport Scotland and ScotRail, and when the Fife Circle commuter train contract came up for renewal, which at that time was still with DB Schenker and Class 67s, it was awarded to DRS, with the Class 68s used from April 2015. (Martin Taylor)**

Fife Circle loco-hauled sets were crewed with DRS drivers and two ScotRail conductors, with one extra to assist with unstaffed station dispatch, useful on the curved platforms on the route. Performances on the services were often very lively, the crews enjoying the opportunity for faster running on passenger services with the high power and acceleration available with the Class 68s.

From the beginning of the loco-hauled services a range of coaching stock was used, though all complying with the hire arrangement specifications of Mk 2 air-conditioned stock. The early use of maroon-liveried EWS coaches, previously hired to Great Western Railway (GWR), led to the nickname 'The Harry Potter Train' by locals. Replacement of this coaching stock, with DB Schenker entering an agreement with Riviera Trains, was received favourably before the DRS (ScotRail-liveried) Mk 2s were introduced when the contract was changed in 2015. In DB Schenker days, there were also occasional Cargo-D hire-ins of Mk 2s when the DBS coaches were under maintenance or refurbishment.

Four of the maroon TSOs were stored at Mossend after replacement – 5631, 5954, 6110 and 6139. When DRS took over the contract for Fife Circle loco-hauled trains, the previously used Mk 2s (11 in total) were stored at Thornton Junction before transfer into storage at Burton and Eastleigh. These comprised: Burton – 3292 2F FO 5657 2D TSO, 3279 2F FO, 3318 2F FO 3331, 2F FO, 3358 2F FO 3400 2F FO and 3424 2F FO. Eastleigh Works – 5632 2D TSO, 9494 2D BSO, 9522 2F BSO.

The two rakes of stock in use at the end of 2018 were reported as:

2F TSOs – 5955, 6027, 5987, 6183, 2D BSO 9488, 2F BSO 9539
2F TSOs – 6177, 6176, 5976, 5952, 5965, 2F BSO 9527

Some negative comments had been received in the local press regarding the use of 1970s Mk 2 coaching stock, and longer point-to-point times for the loco-hauled stock compared to DMUs, though the stock

**On 15 May 2015, 68002** *Intrepid* **waits at Edinburgh Waverley with the full Fife Circle turn: 2G13, the 17.08 Edinburgh–Glenrothes with Thornton arriving at 18.13, then carrying on forward (clockwise around the circle) with 2K14, the 18.14 Glenrothes with Thornton–Edinburgh Waverley, arriving back into the Scottish capital at 19.31.**

**On 15 May 2015, 68002 *Intrepid* arrives at Edinburgh Waverley with the morning full Fife Circle turn (2K01, the 06.37 Edinburgh – Glenrothes with Thornton, arriving at 07.41, going straight forward as 2G02, the 07.46 Glenrothes with Thornton – Edinburgh arriving at.08.56).**

has been very well received by most commuters, being quieter, more spacious and more comfortable than the Sprinter and Class 170 DMUs they replaced and, in the case of 68s, start-to-stop times were comparable, or even better than the DMUs they stand in for.

On rare occasions, problems with the stock or locos meant that DMUs were substituted, generally formed from Classes 158 or 170, previously also occasionally a Class 156 or two, providing a cramped and uncomfortable journey for the unfortunate regular commuters.

ScotRail attracted some criticism for not using the loco-hauled stock on more intensive diagrams, in addition to the morning and evening peak services. There was also some criticism that there were many miles of empty stock movements associated with provision of the services – though these issues were not down to the TOC and were largely due to the lack of a DVT or DBSO – preventing easy train reversals coupled with the need to service the locos and stock at separate facilities. The locos and stock were maintained at Mossend and Motherwell, though with the 67-hauled services some maintenance was carried out at Millerhill with minor stock maintenance and cleaning also on occasions at Perth. Major exams on the Class 68s required light engine movements to and from Crewe or Carlisle. One good knock-on effect of the large-scale need for empty coaching stock (ECS) movements, for enthusiasts at least, was the added opportunities for photography between Mossend and Motherwell via a variety of routes including Carstairs, Falkirk, Shotts, Cumbernauld and the Edinburgh Suburban line (see diagrams table).

When the Forth Road Bridge was closed for repairs on Friday 4 December 2015, ScotRail put on extra services between Edinburgh/Haymarket and Dunfermline/Cowdenbeath to ease overcrowding (with motorists avoiding long road trips by switching to rail travel). The extra trains, using the stock, locos and crew provided for the Fife Circle services, started from the 7 December. One set of coaches came off the regular DRS-provided Fife Circle diagram (with top-and-tail 68s used to avoid run rounds). DB Schenker provided a second rake for the shuttle service, which ran between Inverkeithing/Dunfermline and Edinburgh Haymarket using top-and-tail Class 67s. Locos working the Bridgexes included 67008 and 67021 on the DBS coaches and the regulars, and 68006 and 68007, on the Fife stock. The diagrams involved six return runs each day with brisk start to stop timings. The road bridge reopened on 23 December.

A 2013 Scottish government paper suggested completion dates for electrification of the Fife Circle were anticipated to be 2028. The introduction of HSTs on internal long-distance services reduced some of the urgent need for electrification on other main lines in Scotland and the Fife Circle moved up the list of priorities for introducing overhead wiring, thought initially to be as early as 2023, though electrification of the Forth Rail Bridge may be a sticking point.

Abellio ScotRail announced, at the start of 2019, that as passenger numbers continue to increase, more peak trains would be formed of six carriages, with off-peak services generally to be formed of three carriages – giving 5,000 extra seats each day.

After electrification is completed in the Central Belt, and all the new Class 385 and HSTs are in service, Class 170s are to be redeployed to the Fife Circle to replace the loco-hauled stock.

The loco-hauled services were unable to continue after 2019 due to the Mk 2 stock not being appropriate for people with reduced mobility (PRM) and also non-compliant with technical specifications for interoperability (TSI) – an EU directive that came into force in 2015 and to which the UK would remain bound, regardless of the Brexit outcome, though due to a lack of replacement units a derogation was made for three months.

The last regular loco-hauled Fife Circle working took place on 20 March 2020, with 68016 *Fearless* on 2K14, the 18:14 Glenrothes with Thornton–Edinburgh. On the following Monday, the emergency Covid timetable came into force and only key workers were allowed to travel on Scotrail services. The final day of loco-hauled Fife services was Friday 29 May 2020 with 68006 *Daring* in action – the Class 68s were replaced by Class 170 Turbostar DMUs, which were made available by the introduction of cascaded Inter7City HSTs.

**On 13 December 2016, 68019 stands at Edinburgh Waverley after working the complete evening Fife Circle trip, this train being the second half; 2K14, the 18.14 Glenrothes with Thornton–Edinburgh Waverley.**

# Chapter 7
# TransPennine Express

## Northern route – Liverpool Lime Street to Scarborough

Soon after their introduction on to Chiltern services there were persistent rumours that the TransPennine Newcastle–Liverpool services were also set to be taken over by a fleet of up to 15 Class 68s hauling converted Class 442 EMUs.

In 2017, First Group announced that TransPennine Express (TPE) was ordering CAF Mk 5a stock for use on some of its services, with a deal agreed with DRS to supply some of its Class 68s for use with the new stock. 68021 *Tireless* was moved from DRS's Crewe Gresty Lane depot to Southampton Docks in November 2017 for onwards shipping to the Velim Test Centre in the Czech Republic for test running with the new CAF Mk 5a coaches. Following extensive testing, including door-interlocking and brake force checks, 68021 was returned to the UK in July 2018. 68019 was also used in the Mk 5A test programme. In August 2021, 68021 became the first of the type to receive TPE livery, applied at DRS's depot in Crewe.

The TPE locomotives have received a number of modifications, initially to enable push-pull operation with the new CAF Mk 5A coaches followed by a number of reliability modifications at Wolverton Works with a new data communication module on the loco to work with the Spanish coaches.

**On 17 January 2023, 68032** *Destroyer* **waits at Manchester Piccadilly with 1U47, the 11.35 to Scarborough. In the adjoining platform (Platform 2), Class 323 323233 awaits departure with 2G12, the 11.33 to Hadfield.**

On 9 September 2019, 68027 *Splendid* stands at Liverpool Lime Street after arrival on 1F74, the 16.34 from Scarborough. In the background stands a still incongruous Class 769 hybrid unit, converted from a former Class 319 used on Thameslink services.

On 15 December 2022, a day heavily disrupted by the previous day's strike (and with another strike day to come the next day), few trains were running on the network. Scarborough train crews provided a skeleton service between the town and York, using 68029 and 68025. Here 68025 stands in the north bay (Platform 2) at York after arriving on 1U64, the 15.48 from Scarborough.

On 25 January 2023, 68029 *Courageous* departs Leeds on 1U47, the 11.35 Manchester Piccadilly–Scarborough service. Unusually, the train was worked from Platform 12D; its usual platform (15) being occupied by a late-running TPE service. In the background, new CAF Class 195 DMU 195132 can be seen waiting to depart on 1B24, the 10.19 Blackpool North–York service.

TPE had agreed to run a Class 68-hauled passenger service before the end of 2017 as a franchise commitment. With little prospect of a workable Mk 5 set available for use, the operator ran a short (reduced) Mk 3 rake, from the 'Pretendolino' (ex-Virgin Trains loco-hauled Mk 3 coaches re-liveried to resemble the Class 390 Pendolino EMUs) set on a short trip – 1Z68, 20.38 Manchester Piccadilly–Manchester Airport, and 1Z69 – 21.12 return, the set hauled by 68003 *Astute* and 68030, top-and-tailed.

On 6 February 2018, 68019 hauled a rake, formed of four of the Pretendolino Mk 3s, from Crewe to Preston and return, the first workings with TPE-liveried 68s. The trains ran as 5Z08, the 10.00 Crewe–Preston and 5Z09, 12.02 return.

Test runs with 68020 and the new TPE Mk 5 stock worked throughout September 2018, working as 3B01, the 05.16 Longsight–Bletchley and return. At the time, the application of TPE livery (with blue can ends rather than the traditional yellow – allowed after changes to Group standards – with high-intensity LED headlights being used to warn trackside staff rather than relying on the previous yellow fronts) was controversial with some commentators, though the striking livery has become popular.

TPE initially sub-leased 14 Class 68s (68019–032) from DRS, to begin use on the core Liverpool Lime Street–Scarborough route via Diggle. Once more, sets arrived and sufficient staff were trained, the loco-hauled sets were intended to be used on Manchester Airport–Redcar Central trains. All TPE services utilise five-car rakes of Mk 5A coaches, with a driving trailer at the opposite end. 68033 and 68034 (both in DRS livery) were added to the TPE pool in April 2020 as back up.

68019 *Brutus* awaits departure with 1U72, the 17.48 to Leeds (via Castleford) on 11 January 2023. The diversion via the former colliery town enables TPE train crews to maintain their track knowledge for use during diversions, and occasionally proves useful when stock or units need to be turned.

68020 arrives at Stalybridge on 17 December 2021 on 1U52, the 12.48 Scarborough–Manchester Piccadilly TPE service.

*Right*: In the middle of the rush hour at Leeds, DRS-liveried TPE standby loco 68034 storms out of the station, the Four-Stroke Caterpillar engine reverberating off the overall roof, causing some confusion and concern among the commuters, while working 1U63, the 15.35 Manchester Piccadilly–Malton on 31 January 2023.

*Below*: On 30 January 2020, 68023 A*chilles* waits at Leeds on a Scarborough–Manchester service.

In July 2019, the continuing delay in introducing the Nova 3 sets led to suggestions that TPE was looking to pull out of the CAF coach contract. Shortly afterwards, on 24 August the loco-hauled services finally started, with 68027 *Splendid* and a full set of Mk 5 coaches working the following diagram:

1F48 05.55 Manchester Victoria–Liverpool Lime Street
1E52 06.56 Liverpool Lime Street–Scarborough
1F62 10.41 Scarborough–Liverpool Lime Street
1E39 13.56 Liverpool Lime Street–Scarborough
1F76 17.44 Scarborough–Liverpool Lime Street
1J63 20.56 Liverpool Lime Street–Stalybridge

Ironically, the 68s are yet to perform such high-mileage diagrams on a daily basis. Full introduction of the TPE fleet into service has not taken place. The original introduction schedule was for commencement in December 2018, (as part of an initial franchise commitment). This was deferred to 2019 following issues with training, and technical difficulties with the new CAF stock.

The following (current) diagrams are valid for TPE (North) Class 68-hauled services running from Monday 12 December 2022 until Saturday 20 May 2023. These diagrams cannot be relied upon to produce a Class 68-hauled train – many services are, at the time of writing, being cancelled, often at short notice, and the trains that run may be formed of Class 185 DMUs. It is best to check Realtime Trains before attempting to travel on, or go out to photograph, any of the services listed.

**On the evening of 30 November 2021, 68027** *Superb* **stands spare under the magnificent station roof at York.**

*Right*: 68033 *The Poppy* arrives at Huddersfield on 11 January 2023, on 1U47, the 11.35 Manchester Piccadilly–Scarborough. The (pre-sandblasting) dark, Satanic mills providing a suitable frame for the photo, and also a good reflective surface for the entertaining engine sounds emanating from the Class 68.

*Below*: 68028 *Resolution* arrives into Manchester Piccadilly on 1U28, the 06.48 Scarborough–Manchester in January 2023. Class 323 323229 waits in the adjoining platform with train 2G08, the 09.33 to Hadfield. The Class 68 would shortly afterwards form 1U39, the 09.35 return to Scarborough. After more than a week of trying, this was the first appearance by the booked traction, a Nova 3 Mk 5a-hauled rake, on this service.

On 22 November 2022, 68022 *Resolution* waits in the sidings at Malton with a full Nova 3 rake of stock. Malton is a useful base for TPE to stable stock for driver training on its Class 68s and Mk 5As.

### Diagram 1 (LO601)
### Monday–Saturday (*italic font* = empty stock train)
*5P05 ECS 02.26 Longsight Car Maintenance Depot–Manchester Piccadilly (arr 02.30)*
1P05 02.42 Manchester Piccadilly–York (arr 05.09)
1U20 05.37 York–Manchester Piccadilly (arr 07.11)
1U31 07.29 Manchester Piccadilly–Stables Scarborough TMD (arr 09.53)
1U84 20.58 Scarborough–York (arr 21.48)
1U83 22.03 York–Stables Scarborough Station (arr 22.53)

### Diagram 2 (LO602)
1U28 06.48 Scarborough–Manchester Piccadilly (arr 09.10)
1U39 09.35 Manchester Piccadilly–Scarborough (arr 11.53)
1U52 12.48 Scarborough–Manchester Piccadilly (arr 15.02)
1U63 15.35 Manchester Piccadilly–Scarborough (arr 17.54)
1U76 18.48 Scarborough–Leeds (arr 20.03)
1U79 20.20 Leeds–Scarborough (Via Castleford) (arr 21.53)
*5U79 22.05 Scarborough–Scarborough TMD (arr 22.10)*

### Diagram 3 (LO603)
*5U36 08.25 Scarborough TMD–Scarborough (arr 08.30)*
1U36 08.45 Scarborough–Manchester Piccadilly (arr 11.02)
1U47 11.35 Manchester Piccadilly–Scarborough (arr 13.53)
1U60 14.48 Scarborough–Manchester Piccadilly (arr 17.12)
1U71 17.30 Manchester Piccadilly–Scarborough (arr 19.53)
1P98 22.45 Scarborough–Manchester Piccadilly (arr 01.43)
*5H98 01.35 Manchester Piccadilly–Ongsight Depot (arr 02.04)*

TransPennine Express

**Diagram 5 (LO605)**
5P07 03.31 Longsight Depot–Manchester Airport (arr 03.47)
1P07 04.30 Manchester Airport–Scarborough (arr 07.05)
1U32 07.48 Scarborough–York (arr 08.38)
1U35 10.03 York–Scarborough (arr 10.53)
*5U35 ECS 11.10 Scarborough–Scarborough TMD (arr 11.15)*
*5U72 ECS 17.30 Scarborough TMD–Scarborough (arr 17.35)*
1U72 17.48 Scarborough–Leeds (via Castleford) (arr 20.03)
1U75 19.34 Leeds–Scarborough (arr 21.53)
1U88 21.48 Scarborough–York (arr 22.38)
1U87 23.03 York–Scarborough (arr 23.53)

**Diagram 6 (LO606)**
1U24 05.46 Scarborough–York (arr 06.36)
1U27 08.03 York–Scarborough (arr 08.55)
1U48 11.48 Scarborough–York (arr 12.38)
1U51 14.03 York–Scarborough (arr 14.53)
1U64 15.48 Scarborough–York (arr 16.38)
1U67 18.03 York–Scarborough (arr 18.53)
*5U67 ECS 19.10 Scarborough–Scarborough TMD (arr 19.15)*

**Diagram 7 (LO607)**
*5U40 09.30 Scarborough TMD–Scarborough (arr 09.35)*
1U40 09.48 Scarborough–York (arr 10.38)
1U43 12.03 York–Scarborough (arr 12.53)
1U56 13.48 Scarborough–York (arr 14.38)
1U59 16.03 York–Scarborough (arr 16.53)
1U80 19.48 Scarborough–Manchester Piccadilly (arr 22.25)
*5U80 22.37 Manchester Piccadilly–Longsight Depot (arr 22.49)*

**On 15 December 2022, 68029 stands in Scarborough with a (nowadays) very rare several inches of snow on the ground. This service was provided on an ad hoc basis on non-strike days during the railway's industrial dispute.**

On 11 November 2022, 68029 stands at Scarborough with 1F68, the 13.34 to York.

Scarborough is one of the few stations in the country where platforms allowed disembarkation from both sides of arriving trains – a feature made necessary by the large numbers of passengers arriving on the many summer excursions and on additional services arriving at this formerly very popular tourist location.

Nowadays, with much lower passenger numbers, and central door locking means that doors are opened on one side of the train.

On 11 January 2023, 68033 *The Poppy* awaits departure with 1P98, the 22.45 to Manchester Piccadilly, a train that has been regularly cancelled by TPE and once again on this evening ran as a bus service. Alongside, 68031 *Felix* stands spare.

## Southern Route–Liverpool Lime Street–Cleethorpes

While Class 68s have been fairly regular visitors to Cleethorpes for a number of years (on occasional excursions and on test and rail head treatment trains) the next few years should see the type become an everyday sight on the route, taking over the main TPE services to and from Manchester Piccadilly, hauling CAF Mk 5 stock (The 'Nova 3' sets).

September 2021 saw the first plans to use Class 68s on through Liverpool–Cleethorpes services for TransPennine Express, on its Nova3 CAF Mk 5-hauled services (replacing Class 185 DMUs and giving the prospect of regular loco-hauled services into Cleethorpes for the first time since 1988. The planned introduction date of December 2021 slipped, initially to mid-2022, then to December 2022, due to delays to the crew-training schedule, and there were doubts that the December timetable change would see a smooth introduction into traffic (with ongoing problems with the Nova 3 fleet on Scarborough trains and frequent cancellations). Those doubts were well founded, and as of March 2023 very few Class 68s have gone on to work service trains in and out of Cleethorpes, though crew training with empty stock workings continue.

As part of the training programme, the first full Nova 3 set with Mk 5A coaches ran empty to Scarborough on 25 January 2019, pushed across the Pennines from Manchester by 68028 *Lord President*.

Light engine test runs began in January 2022 with 68034 doing out-and-back trips from York.

Monday 12 December 2022 was the first official timetabled day for Class 68 operations to Cleethorpes, with the town covered in freezing fog for the duration. Three different cab designs were visible by the buffer stops on platforms 2–4 (Platform 2 nearest the camera). In order, 68020 on the training set (after working the first services over the previous Thursday–Saturday in lieu of training runs), 185108 standing spare and Driving Trailer 12805 on a Mk 5A set, led by 68026, also spare after arriving earlier from Manchester.

A different view of the cab fronts on view at Cleethorpes on Monday 12 December 2022.

On Monday 19 December 2022, 68028 *Lord President* waits at Cleethorpes on a rake of Mk 5 stock. The set was due to head back to Manchester on the 15.24, but a lack of train crew saw the train replaced by a bus service and the Nova 3 set returned empty to Doncaster later that evening.

By November 2022 a regular training diagram was being operated daily with a TPE Class 68 and Nova 3 stock (Doncaster Europort, sometimes referred to as Doncaster International Railport, is an intermodal rail terminal, conveniently sited near the M18/A1 road junction in the yard complexes south of the station). Prior to October 2022 these empty, driver-training runs ran to Doncaster Belmont Down Yard in the evenings.

5A22 09.32 Doncaster Europort–Cleethorpes (arr 11.07)
5B73 09.26 Cleethorpes–Manchester Piccadilly (arr 12.11)
5B78 13.18 Manchester Piccadilly–Cleethorpes (arr 15.53)
5A23 16.10 Cleethorpes–Doncaster (arr 17.45)

Provisional passenger diagrams were published unofficially in October 2022 in advance of the hoped-for introduction of the 68s on the Cleethorpes route.

## The South Route
**Diagram 1**
5B60 05.11 Doncaster Europort–Doncaster (arr 05.32)
1B60 05.37 Doncaster–Cleethorpes (arr 06.50)
1B69 07.27 Cleethorpes–Liverpool LS (arr 11.00)
1B76 11.19 Liverpool LS–Cleethorpes (arr 14.53)
1B85 15.24 Cleethorpes–Liverpool LS (arr 19.01)
5H85 19.27 Liverpool LS–Stables Longsight (arr 21.28)

**Diagram 2**
5B64 04.32 Longsight–Manchester Air (arr 05.19)
1B64 05.43 Manchester Air–Cleethorpes (arr 08.53)
1B73 09.26 Cleethorpes–Liverpool LS (arr 13.00)
1B80 13.19 Liverpool LS–Cleethorpes (arr 16.52)
1B89 17.24 Cleethorpes–Liverpool LS (arr 21.00)
1B96 21.19 Liverpool LS–Doncaster (arr 23.54)
5B96 00.06 Doncaster–Doncaster Europort (arr 00.25)

Thursday 8 December 2022 finally saw the first timetabled Class 68 passenger workings over the Cleethorpes Line with 68020 working the following trains on Thursday 8 December, Friday 9 December and Saturday 10 December, in advance of the planned introduction of the new timetable a few days later:

5A22 06.20 Doncaster Europort–Cleethorpes (arr 08.00)
1B73 09.26 Cleethorpes–Manchester Piccadilly (arr 12.01)
1B78 13.18 Manchester Piccadilly–Cleethorpes (arr 15.52)
5A23 21.51 Cleethorpes–Doncaster Europort (arr 23.12)

Starting on Monday 12 December, five Class 68s and Mk 5 stock were allocated to the Liverpool and Manchester International Airport–Cleethorpes route, though only two sets were booked in traffic each day, with each set booked to work one single passenger service; the rest of the sets and diagrams allow for spare stock, empty stock workings/training runs at Gascoigne Wood Sidings (formerly used by coal traffic for the now-closed adjacent mine, and latterly as a loading point for Gypsum products, and also a storage site for withdrawn rolling stock, including Class 142s and HSTs) or on maintenance at Longsight Depot. Two sidings are also available to TPE for storage of full sets of Class 68s and Mk 5As at Freightliner's Doncaster Europort facility.

Diagrams are as follows (italic font = empty stock working):

**LO609**
*5B64 04.32 Longsight Carriage MD–Manchester Airport (arr 05.19)*
1B64 05.43 Manchester Airport–Cleethorpes (arr 08.53)
*5B73 09.26 Cleethorpes–Liverpool (arr 13.00)*
*5B80 13.19 Liverpool–Cleethorpes (arr 16.52)*
*5B99 22.36 Cleethorpes–Doncaster (arr 23.58)*
*5D99 00.06 Doncaster–Doncaster Railport (arr 00.23)*

**LO610**
*5B60 05.06 Doncaster Railport–Cleethorpes (arr 06.45)*
1B85 15.24 Cleethorpes–Liverpool (arr 19.01)
*5H85 19.27 Liverpool–Longsight Carriage MD (arr 22.08)*

**LO611**
Gascoigne Wood Sidings stabled/spare

**68020** *Reliance* **stands in Platform 2 at Cleethorpes on the training set on Monday 12 December 202, before working 1B85, the 15.24 to Liverpool Lime Street, terminating this day at Manchester Piccadilly.**

**LO612**
Gascoigne Wood Sidings stabled/spare

**LO613**
Longsight maintenance/exam

Longer term, the Class 68s may not have a secure future on TPE services, with the operating company seeking expressions of interest for up to 30 bi-mode locomotives earlier in 2022, with an option for five more for use on the Great Western Railway Night Riviera sleeper.

In January 2022, First Group announced that it had issued a tender for up to 30 new bi-mode locomotives with a minimum of 15 to be allocated for TPE use (to replace the 15 Beacon-owned Class 68s, currently sub-leased from DRS).

The new locomotives will be able to take advantage of the extended overhead electrification being introduced as part of the railway's drive towards zero carbon, while still maintaining sufficient diesel power for working over slower unelectrified routes (such as Scarborough and Cleethorpes).

It is possible that the new locos may be a follow-on order to the Class 99s being built for ROG and GBRf, giving even more variety along the Lincolnshire coast line.

**68020 waits at Sheffield in the remains of a brief snowstorm on 22 December 2022, working the first official loco-hauled TPE Southern Pennine service to Manchester Piccadilly, on the first day of the new timetable. The train was 1B85, the 15.24 to Liverpool Lime Street, terminating this day at Manchester Piccadilly.**

68033 is seen shoving 1T29 11.00 York–Scarborough TPE 'shuttle' away from York, passing the apple-laden allotments and terraced houses near the Nestle factory at Crichton Avenue on 3 August 2020. The Scarborough shuttles were implemented as the country got back on its feet after the first wave of Covid. No one expected they would continue for more than two years. (Martin Taylor)

68033 *The Poppy* arrives at Seamer on 17 January 2023 working 1U56, the 13.48 Scarborough–York, with the remains of a very heavy frost clinging on in the shadows.

# Chapter 8
# Railtours and Heritage Diesel Galas

When they first appeared, the Class 68s were eagerly sought out by enthusiasts. Consequently, they were much in demand for railtours and appearances at galas on preserved railways.

The first appearance by a member of the class at a heritage event took place on the Mid-Norfolk Railway when 68007 *Valiant* was provided by DRS for the Christmas Diesel Gala of 2014 between 27 and 28 December. The loco worked between Dereham and Wymondham Abbey, with a rake of Mk 2 (ETH-capable) stock and 45133 ensuring that passengers were kept warm during the out-of-season event. The loco also worked some services solo.

The Spring 2016 Severn Valley Diesel Gala, held between 19 and 21 May, saw 68025 *Superb* visiting; as the latest delivered member of the class, this was a big draw at the event, the loco being used to a haul another visitor – an ex-Southern Region 4TC set (due to the lack of suitable air-braked stock among Severn Valley's own collection). The high profile visit was marred by the shameful theft of the loco's builder plate, stolen while it was on shed at Bewdley on the night of 21 May, though this was eventually returned, though not till the start of June the following year following DRS's threats to withdraw its locomotives from future events.

## Freight duties

While the workings of the Class 68s on passenger duties have attracted the most publicity, the type is a true mixed traffic locomotive. In addition to passenger duties, DRS has used the class on a wide range of freight traffic including multimodal services, ballast trains (on a contract with Network Rail), occasional appearances on the Venice Simplon-Orient Express Northern Belle trains and assorted freight traffic (including some nuclear flask trains).

Initially the class saw use on freight in Scotland, concentrated on multimodal duties, with relatively few appearances south of the border save for a few Network Rail special workings between Crewe Basford Hall and Toton (often short trains of autoballasters), and occasional runs between Daventry and Mossend on liner trains.

The freight workings that saw most Class 68 use initially (as part of the acceptance trials for the locos) were Network Rail-operated Crewe–Mountsorrel and Carlisle workings:

6C18 02.52 Crewe Basford Hall–Carlisle Yard
6K27 15.06 Carlisle Yard–Crewe Basford Hall
6U76 08.59 Crewe Basford Hall–Mountsorrel (empty IOAs – Network Rail high-sided bogie box wagons, built by Greenbrier in 2009)
6U77 13.57 Mountsorrel–Crewe Basford Hall (loaded IOAs)

The Mountsorrel duty, in particular, has been a long-standing regular for Class 68s with Network Rail-operated ballast hopper traffic (from Lafarge's large quarry at the Leicestershire site), many locomotives being tested and run in on such trains.

Newly introduced 68002 appeared on 4A13, the 12.20 Grangemouth–Aberdeen WH Malcolm container service on Sunday 28 December 2014, seen here near Fouldubs Junction at the start of its journey. This flow, which ended in November 2021 with 68006 doing the honours, could produce either a Class 66 or 68 as traction, and when a 68, was often swapped around with the two locos on the ScotRail Fife Circle diagrams when exams were needed. (Martin Taylor)

On 28 May 2014, 68004 was used to haul multimodal service 6Z76, Crewe Basford Hall–Willesden Euroterminal as far as Daventry with 47805 and 66426 dead inside for insurance purposes. Two days later, the same loco ran light engine as 0Z68 Crewe Gresty Bridge–Daventry to work 4S44, the 12.05 Daventry International Rail Freight Terminal (DIRFT)–Coatbridge as far as Crewe, with 66433 dead in tow.

On 2 June, the 68 worked the train north as far as Carlisle. From the end of June 2014, 68003 was based at DRS Motherwell for training purposes in advance of the use of 68s on Scottish intermodal services. Training runs were made to and from Grangemouth before their start in service on 29 July, with 68005 on 4H47, the 05.14 from Mossend to Inverness 'Stobart' service; the train starting 20 minutes late but after a sparkling run, arriving into Inverness 77 minutes early. The class went on to a number of additional freight workings and Scottish multimodal traffic including.

The Mossend to Inverness 'Tesco' liner workings became a regular duty for the class. Stobart Rail, together with DRS launched the service in 2009, helping remove much lorry traffic from the vital A9 trunk road through the Central Highlands, the longest road in Scotland, with its most important section running between Perth and Inverness. Haulage was taken over by DB Schenker Class 66s between 4 January 2010, but returned to DRS on 25 April 2011 with Class 66s, and later Class 68s, taking over the duties.

Trains operated are:

(Loaded) 4H47, 05.08 Mossend Up Yard–Inverness DRS Freight Sidings (arr 10.57)
(Empties) 4D47 13.19 Inverness DRS Freight Sidings–Mossend Up Yard (arr 17.56)
4A13 12.20 Grangemouth–Aberdeen Craiginches
4N83 18.20 Aberdeen Craiginches–Grangemouth

24 September 2014 saw the first appearance by a silver Chiltern-liveried example in Scotland when 68014 was sent north from Kingmoor, after maintenance, to work 4H47 north from Mossend.

After a return to DRS Class 66 haulage for a period on 2 June 2015, 68005 appeared on 4H47 and 4D47.

On 15 July 2015, the Inverness 'Tesco' service saw a pair of Class 68s with 68001 *Evolution* and 68003 *Astute* provided by DRS from Mossend on 4H47 with 68001 working the southbound service singly and 68003 returning south by assisting 66304 on 6Z25, an additional 11.15 Inverness–Carlisle Yard engineers' train.

In 2015, DRS Class 68s also made regular appearances on the Grangemouth to Aberdeen intermodal workings. On 15 July, 68005 was noted working 4A13, the 12.23 Grangemouth–Aberdeen Craiginches and 4N83 18.20 return.

These workings largely reverted to Class 66s from 2017 and on 14 November 68033 was used, the first time for six months, following the failure of 66431 the previous day. ScotRail-liveried 68006 *Daring* worked the 4H47 on 2 June 2018, a first for the type for three months.

DRS also provides Class 68s for Network Rail testing, engineering and infrastructure duties. From 2017 onwards the last of the freshly arrived Class 68s were occasionally run in on an out-and-back ballast working from Carlisle to Mountsorrel or Bescot, the train pairs being:

6M36 00.44 Carlisle Yard–Mountsorrel (empty ballast)
6C89 09.45 Mountsorrel–Carlisle Yard (loaded ballast)

68003 became the first Class 68 to work under power over the Cumbrian line on 30 January 2015, beginning the type's long associations with the route, working a circular light engine driver-training run from Carlisle Kingmoor via Whitehaven, the Dalton loop and back via Shap (over the West Coast Main Line).

By February 2015, DRS had enough Class 68s available for traffic to be able to end its hire agreement with DBS for Class 92s to work 4S43, the 12.05 Daventry–Mossend 'Tesco' liner service. The first day of Class 68 operation was 6 February with 68007 *Valiant* and 68004 *Rapid* noted in charge. Class 68s continued to make regular appearances on the services up until September 2016, though have returned to the duties more recently, working in pairs in place of the previous Class 88s.

2015 saw the fleet continue to spread out, with a number of longer distance workings including on 8 June when 68015 hauled two PFA wagons on 6Z70, the 05.43 Willesden Brent–Eastleigh Works. Another ballast working occasionally worked by Class 68s is:

6C27 09.42 Carlisle Yard–Shap Summit
6C28 15.20 Shap Summit–Carlisle Yard

On 28 September, Chiltern silver-liveried 68010 found its way north to Carlisle in charge of 6C18 02.52 Basford Hall–Carlisle Yard empty MHA service, working straight back south the same day on 6K27, 15.06 off Carlisle, with the loaded return service.

Less common engineers' train workings for the type have included occasional trips between York and Doncaster with 68001 *Evolution* noted on 4 January 2016 on 6Z51, a 13.55 York Works–Doncaster Decoy, returning to York the following day.

While the non-passenger locomotives (68001–68007 and 68016–68019) have worked most of the freight turns associated with the class, the TPE and Chiltern-liveried examples have been used on a few such workings, often on Network Rail associated flows. In late 2022, with continuing difficulties introducing the full Nova 3 fleet into service, a number of TPE Class 68s began to be seen on freight duties, notably the circular diagram:

  6G94 12.22 Crewe Basford Hall–Bescot
  6D95 14.41 Bescot–Toton
  6K97 19.33 Toton–Crewe Basford Hall

Unusually, on 21 and 22 November 2022, Chiltern-liveried 68015 *Kev Helmer* was used on the 12.22 Crewe Basford Hall–Bescot (though this was a positional move to move the loco back south after maintenance, ready to return to passenger duties with Chiltern).

Another good turn for a Class 68 on freight is 6K05, the 12.41 Carlisle Yard to Crewe Basford Hall departmental service, routed via the Settle and Carlisle Line and giving excellent photographic opportunities to see this pleasing design on one of England's most scenic lines. This service is also routed via the West Coast Main Line on occasions, giving further good photo choices in areas such as Tebay and Shap.

# Chapter 9
# Special Traffic

The autumn and winter of 2016 saw the first use of DRS Class 68s on Railhead Treatment Trains (RHTT) work, with 37716 and 68003 substituting for the more usual pair of DRS Class 20s, working in top-and-tail mode on the South Yorkshire circuit on 29 October – noted on the 09.50 Worksop–Stocksbridge.

Class 68s have since been used widely for RHTT work where DRS has supplied the traction. These have included turns along the Cumbrian Coast, such as the circular run starting on 3J11, the 11.29 Carlisle Kingmoor–Whitehaven, then back to Carlisle, over the West Coast Main Line to Carnforth, the Little North and Western to Settle Junction, up the Settle and Carlisle Line to Blea Moor, back south on to Barrow via Wennington, then back to Carlisle Kingmoor at 06.20 the following morning.

On 19 October 2019, 68005 made a rare appearance at Grimsby on the Lincolnshire Coast RHTT after the failure of booked traction 20305 and 20303, the two locos causing delays by blocking the bay platform for services from Newark and Lincoln.

Another Class 68 RHTT duty has been 6Z77, the 06.45 Carlisle Kingmoor–Tyne Yard (via Carstairs and Morpeth) and 6K05, the 12.46 Carlisle Yard–Crewe Basford Hall.

**Due to heavily contaminated railheads on the Tyne Valley Line between Hexham and Newcastle, 3J77/3J78 Kingmoor–Nunthorpe and return NE07 RHTT circuit was requisitioned by Network Rail control to carry out an additional pass over this section (twice instead of once) on 15 November 2021. Traction on this day was 68018 and 88005, and here a dirty 68018** *Vigilant* **leads the second pass (as train 3J79) jetting through a very autumnal and damp Riding Mill shortly after 14.00. (Martin Taylor)**

## Nuclear traffic

Class 68s have been closely associated with some of DRS's core traffic of nuclear flask transfer. Since the opening of the world's first nuclear power station at Calder Hall (Sellafield) in 1956, the transport of nuclear material has been a sensitive issue. It soon became clear that rail movement of this material was the safest and most practical option.

British Rail (BR) originally used well wagons (designed to carry large, heavy items such as transformers or other heavy machinery) until special insulated flasks were introduced in 1960, built by BR at its Shildon Works. The familiar XKB (later redesignated FNA) flasks were introduced in 1969 and were in service until recent times, but were replaced with the newer modernised FNA-D type, constructed by WH Davis of Shirebrook, between 2014 and 2019. Larger, even more secure flasks (designated KUA) are also in use for Ministry of Defence traffic, together with Mk 2 support coaches.

Nuclear waste is transported from British power stations to and from Sellafield, with some freight generated by the import of material from Italy, Japan and Switzerland through the Channel Tunnel or into Ramsden Dock (Barrow in Furness). From the late 1950s until 1971, nuclear rail freight operations were controlled by the UK Atomic Energy Authority, transferring that year to British Nuclear Fuels Ltd (BNFL) until the Nuclear Decommissioning Agency took charge of overseeing operations from 2005.

Operations for the nuclear freight traffic began with BR before transferring to EWS upon privatisation. (From the 1980s, the Railfreight coal sector took over responsibility). The political sensitivity of the movement of potentially hazardous material saw the government form Direct Rail Services (DRS) in 1994, in order to operate nuclear fuel-related traffic. The owner is British Nuclear Fuels (BNFL), ostensibly remaining state-owned due to the political sensitivity of operating potentially hazardous nuclear freight flows within the private sector). DRS's main bases are Carlisle and Crewe with a smaller maintenance site based at Sellafield.

Until 1998, DRS had limited traffic, mostly flows of imported fuel for reprocessing at BNFLs Sellafield plant, from that year taking over nuclear flask traffic – the movement of nuclear waste for storage and/or reprocessing (again at Sellafield) from sites including Berkeley, Bridgewater, Dungeness, Heysham, Hunterston, Seaton, Sizewell and Valley.

By 2000, DRS's heritage fleet of diesel locomotives, including Classes 20, 37 and 47, were becoming increasingly unreliable as well as expensive to maintain. One option was to expand the company's Class 66 fleet, though it was recognized that even the relatively new Class 66 didn't comply with the latest emissions' regulations from the European Union. In addition, the 66 wasn't very fuel efficient, was without head-end power (electric train supply) and had a maximum speed of 120km/h (75mph). It couldn't readily be hired out for regular timetabled passenger operations, or charter work.

With few other options at the time, in October 2003 DRS signed a contract for the purchase of 34 Class 66s, later expanded to 39, mainly for freight work. From 2008 onwards, DRS also began to acquire Class 57s including no-heat 57/0s and ex-Virgin Thunderbird 57/3s.

The nuclear power plant at Wylfa on Anglesey provided much flask traffic along the North Wales Coast with 68s featuring strongly in more recent years. The first Class 68 on this traffic was on 8 May 2017 when 68003 *Astute*, paired with Class 57 57305 *Northern Princess* on 6D43, the 07.36 Crewe CLS–Valley, returning on 6K41, the 14.58 Valley–Crewe CLS.

The last run of the flask trains along the North Wales Coast took place on 18 September 2018. The 6D43/07.31 Crewe CLS–Valley NE and its return duty as the 6K41/14.57 from Valley was handled by 68005 and 68033. In total, 26 different members of the type were recorded on the Valley flasks.

Up until early 2017, it was common for DRS's 'heritage' traction to work alongside 68s on flask traffic, and for mixed pairs of locos to be used on nuclear flask and Ministry of Defence flask trains. A steer from the higher echelons of management then insisted that in the majority of cases, the Class 68s (and 88s as they came on stream) were to be used wherever possible and the older fleet dispensed with, either via disposal or to other traffic. This almost instantly removed views such as this of a fairly new 68025 *Superb* sandwiched between 37259 and 37423 on 6C46, the 19.31 Sellafield BNF–Carlisle Kingmoor flask trip skirting the wall at Tanyard Bay, Parton, on the evening of 30 May 2016. (Martin Taylor)

68005 *Defiant* and 37607 are seen working 6C46 19.31 Sellafield BNF–Carlisle Kingmoor flask curving away from Harrington towards Moss Bay in good evening light on 23 May 2016. This was a great location to shoot this train as well as the evening 2C47 Barrow–Carlisle Class 37-hauled Northern passenger service, though the coastal erosion was strongly evident and on almost every visit, another section of the footpath had fallen away to the rocky beach below. (Martin Taylor)

The Hinkley Point Nuclear Power plant near Bridgwater in Somerset also generates regular trainloads for DRS with a train pair running regularly:

6V74 02.00 Crewe CLS–Bridgewater
6M63 11.58 Bridgewater–Crewe CLS

Torness Nuclear Power Plant is situated on a short branch off the East Coast Main Line south of Oxwellmains (near Dunbar in East Lothian, southeast of Edinburgh) and generates some rail traffic from waste materials for reprocessing, trains running as:

6S43 06.23 Carlisle Kingmoor–Torness NPS
6M50 15.07 Torness NPS–Carlisle Kingmoor

The UK Atomic Energy site at Winfrith saw Class 68s head to Hampshire with occasional waste traffic, often running as 6Z62 01.03 Crewe CLS–Winfrith. The site was decommissioned in 2021, ending such traffic.

Nearer to their home base at Kingmoor, Class 68s are also used on the relatively short trips from Heysham Harbour to and from Sellafield. On 25 May 2017, 68027 and 68002 *Intrepid* worked 6C51, the 12.58 Sellafield–Heysham Harbour and returning on 6C52, the 16.19 Heysham Harbour–Sellafield. Flask traffic is also operated between Sellafield and Crewe with two trains 6K73, the 08.49 Sellafield–Crewe and 6C53, the 06.25 Crewe–Sellafield.

From 2022, Class 68s have also been seen on the Far North Line on nuclear flask traffic for Dungeness B nuclear power station, working 6S99, the 05.21 Carlisle Kingmoor–Georgemass Junction.

68s have occasionally stood in for Class 66s and Class 88s on multimodal traffic on the West Coast Main Line. Where they have replaced 88s, they are often paired up to maintain the scheduled timings for the powerful AC electrics.

Liner services worked have included:

6L48 14.08 Garston–Dagenham Dock
6L47 22.48 Garston Car Terminal–Dagenham Dock.

One spectacular Class 68 working took place in the summer of 2017 with 6C53, the 06.30 Crewe Coal Sidings–Sellafield often featuring four locomotives with 68025 and 68023 and 68005 and 68020 recorded on 1 June hauling the service, with 68005 and 68030 and 68017 and 68023 noted on 22 June, and 68029 and 68022 and 68001 and 68030 on 29 June.

In 2017, 6D43, the 07.36 Crewe–Valley nuclear flasks and 6K41, 14.58 return, were noted with pairs of Class 68s, running on Mondays, Wednesdays and Fridays, with 68001/03–05/16/17/20/22/23/25/26/28/30 all noted.

In the summer of 2017, the Dungeness branch was cleared for Class 68s, with nuclear flask traffic from Crewe taken over by Class 68s. The first 68-hauled working on 12 September, was 6O62, the 01.03 Crewe Coal Sidings (DRS)–Dungeness British Energy, returning as 6M95, the 16.40 Dungeness British Energy–Crewe Coal Sidings (DRS) and featured 68002 and 68033, with 68003 and 69018 working on 19 September, and 68017 and 68032 on 2 October.

Another rare working is the (generally) annual low-level radioactive waste service from Carlisle to Hull (via the Tyne Valley and ECML), seen on 16 November 2017, top-and-tailed by 68034 and 68004.

## Test trains

From the beginning of 2016, DRS has hired Class 68s to Network Rail for use on the Derby RTC-based test trains, generally in top-and-tail mode. The debut for the class took place on 12 January 2016 when 68016 *Fearless* and 68004 *Rapid* worked 1Q18, the 08.23 Derby RTC–Heaton, and on 18 January a longer round trip, again beginning with a Derby to Heaton run, but carrying on to Millerhill and Craigentinny and heading back south via Skipton and Bradford Forster Square. The test trains saw 68s continue to break new grounds for the type, with 68002 and 68004 making a trip to East Anglia on 22 February 2016 on an 1Q18 Derby to Ely via Cambridge and London Liverpool Street working, again in top-and-tail mode. On 15 February, 68004 *Rapid* and 68017 *Hornet* took the track recording coaches to London Euston station and the following day worked from Crewe to Mossend via Dumfries, Ayr and Glasgow Central before returning to Crewe on 17 February.

On 1 April 2016, 68002 *Intrepid* and 68004 *Rapid* top-and-tailed a test train through to London Paddington and Swansea.

On 30 June 2016, 68004 *Rapid* and 68020 *Reliance* worked 1Q23, an 04.56 Old Oak Common to Salisbury test train, the first and only time that the Class has travelled west of Salisbury on the Waterloo–Exeter Line, the class not being passed for the route and gaining a one-day derogation only.

## Random workings

Class 68s have occasionally made appearances as rescue locos. On 29 October 2015, after transporting newly arrived 68016 and 68017 from Workington Docks to Carlisle, 68004 *Rapid* was scrambled to rescue Colas Class 60 60096 on 6C37, the 22.25 Chirk–Carlisle Yard timber empties after the 60 failed near Tebay, the Class 68 dragging the train forward to Kingmoor.

On 16 June, 68024 made an extremely rare and unusual appearance, dragging Class 320 EMUs 320411 and 320412, which had become stranded on 2B95, the 23.52 Lanark–Motherwell due to overhead wire problems, the 68 working between Wishaw and Motherwell.

On 2 July 2016, 68009 was called to assist a failed Freightliner Class 70 (70006) working 4S44, the 12.13 Daventry–Coatbridge, the 68 hauling the service from Brinklow to Crewe Basford Hall, where 70004 was summoned to take the service forwards.

While London Liverpool Street to Norwich services still utilised Mk 3s and Class 90s, Class 68s were hired for occasional use, tripping stock between Norwich and Bounds Green or Wolverton Works. On 3 February 2016, 68004 *Rapid* was noted with two Mk 3 coaches (12125/9) on a train from Norwich to Bounds Green.

The Class 68s based at Norwich for Wherry Line and standby duties were occasionally used by Greater Anglia on other duties, as on 15 July 2016, when 68019 was provided to haul a failed 90005 as 5P30 empties from London Liverpool Street back to Norwich Crown Point depot.

On 25 October, with Liverpool Street services in a state of disarray, Greater Anglia organised a relief service at short notice, utilising the Wherry Lines 'short set' and running as 1G33, the 11.50 Norwich to Colchester, featuring 68004 and 68024 in the usual top-and-tail mode on the rake, returning to Norwich as 1P34, the 14.47 from Colchester.

26 October saw 68002 used to drag failed 90005 back to Norwich from Diss after the 90 failed on 1P47, the 15.00 Norwich to London Liverpool Street.

68005 and 68018 were used between Barrow Docks Marine Terminal and Sellafield on 9 May 2016, working a series of test runs in top-and-tail mode with a mixed formation of Mk 2 coaches and flat wagons. The train returned to Carlisle later in the afternoon.

Another highly unusual working took place on 28 July 2016 when 68023 worked 6Z78, the 10.10 Whitemoor–Hoo Junction, which ran over the North Kent Line via Dartford.

*Left*: On 16 September 2017, 68034 awaits departure from London Liverpool Street with 1G04, the 16.24 to Norwich as part of a charity railtour to commemorate the end of diesel locos with Greater Anglia services. 68001 *Evolution* was at the rear of the set.

*Below*: 68034 hauls failed classmate 68025 *Superb* and TP07 set past Low Moor Meadows (Morley) on 5Z60 10.10 Scarborough–Crewe Basford Hall. 68025 had failed at Scarborough station five days prior, and recovery was delayed. The top of Leeds city centre landmark Bridgwater Place is visible just above the leading loco. 68025 was later tripped on to DRS's site at Gresty (Crewe) for fault finding. (Martin Taylor)

68002 worked to Ripple Lane on 10 August 2018 on 4L48, the 13.53 from Daventry and two days later it worked 4V38, the 09.12 Daventry–Wentloog Stobart intermodal.

11 August 2016 saw 68022 work an additional 6Z69 15.18 Slateford–Carlisle Kingmoor, a train comprising two stoneblowers, which continued its journey as 6Z70, the 21.00 Kingmoor–Horsham Yard, reportedly the first revenue-earning Class 68 service, into Sussex.

With the protracted delay in introducing Class 68s, TPE used the ex-Virgin Pretendolino rake of Mk 3s as part of its training programme (in the absence of the new Mk 5 stock). On 24 November 2016, 68024 *Centaur*, running as 5Z69, the 10.03 Norwich–Laira, moved the set for refurbishment work after the cessation of a hire agreement for use of the stock with Greater Anglia but in the end TPE never used the stock in everyday regular service following discussions with the DfT and Rail North Partnership, due to the Mk 3s not meeting disability regulations.

# Chapter 10
# Names, Models and the Future

## Names and the naming policy
Despite sub-leasing the locomotives to passenger operators, mainly Chiltern and TPE, DRS has been in charge of the naming policy for the Class 68 fleet. The names chosen are shown in the fleet list table. DRS is strongly rumoured to have planned a different series of names for the later deliveries of locomotives (to be sub-leased for use by TPE) with these thought to have included *Nautilus* (68026), *Endeavour* (68027), *Splendid* (68028), *Destroyer* (68029), *Enterprise* (68030), *Excelsior* (68031), *Patriot* (68032), *Courageous* (68033) and *Victorious* (68034). TPE was thought to have overruled these proposals, choosing names such as *Lord President* for 68028 (following a strong railway tradition of use of the name that most recently appeared on Class 87 87028. Despite the fleet featuring many warship names, including several previously used on locomotives, including Class 50s, DRS denied that there was a naval theme to its naming policy.

## Models
The popularity of the Class 68 locomotive has been reflected in the range of model railway versions produced, in both OO (1:76 Scale) and N gauges. The OO gauge version was released as a ready-to-run DCC fitted loco with 21 pin sockets in 2017 with 18-pin N gauge versions made available the following year. In July 2014, Dapol laser-scanned 68005 at DRS's Carlisle Kingmoor Depot with the resulting 3D file being sent to China, in advance of N gauge and OO gauge models being released in 2016.

Dapol bought the licence to be the designated manufacturer for Class 68 models, with some excellent versions produced, taking advantage of the latest 3D laser measuring and computer aided design and production – enabling the company to sell some very detailed and realistic working models.

Versions of the locos in DRS, Scotrail, Chiltern and TransPennine Express liveries are available in both N and OO gauges with the latest five-pole smooth motors, directional lighting and all-wheel pickup ensuring very smooth running. Sound-fitted versions are also available.

## Class 68s, the future
With 68006 modified to run on lower carbon fuel, and with the government certain to press for lower carbon rail use, it appears that the work for the fleet on freight duties is secured for the immediate future. The use of Class 68s on passenger duties is less certain. Loco-hauled passenger trains are set to end with Chiltern over the course of the next year as maintenance on the Mk 3 stock has been ramped down, and the use of 68s on TPE trains has not seen full utilisation of the fleet, with the prospect of electrification seeing perhaps electric locomotives used in preference in the future.

At the time of writing there are strong rumours (from senior sources within DRS) that the Welsh government (through Transport for Wales) is keen to replace Class 67s currently seeing use with Mk IV stock on Swansea/Cardiff to Manchester/Holyhead with Class 68s, with those locos soon to be replaced by Chiltern as the obvious replacements.

We await developments with interest.

# Class 68 Fleet Table

| Loco | Name | Works Number | Delivered | Livery | Pool | Operator | Details |
|---|---|---|---|---|---|---|---|
| 68001 | Evolution | 2679 | 29 August 2014 Liverpool | DRS | XHVE | DRS | |
| 68002 | Intrepid | 2680 | 18 January 2014 Southampton | DRS | XHVE | DRS | |
| 68003 | Astute | 2681 | 15 April 2014 Liverpool | DRS | XHVE | DRS | |
| 68004 | Rapid | 2682 | 15 April 2014 Liverpool | DRS | XHVE | DRS | |
| 68005 | Defiant | 2683 | 15 April 2014 Liverpool | DRS | XHVE | DRS | |
| 68006 | Pride of The North | 2684 | 10 June 2014 Liverpool | DRS | XHVE | DRS | Formerly operated by ScotRail with Abellio branding, formerly named Daring |
| 68007 | Valiant | 2685 | 10 June 2014 Liverpool | DRS | XHVE | DRS | Formerly operated by ScotRail with Abellio branding |
| 68008 | Avenger | 2686 | 10 June 2014 Liverpool | DRS | XHVE | DRS/Chiltern Railways | |
| 68009 | Titan | 2687 | 31 July 2014 Liverpool | DRS | XHVE | DRS/Chiltern Railways | |
| 68010 | Oxford Flyer | 2688 | 31 July 2014 Liverpool | Chiltern | XHCE | Chiltern Railways | |
| 68011 | | 2689 | 31 July 2014 Liverpool | Chiltern | XHCE | Chiltern Railways | |
| 68012 | | 2690 | 29 August 2014 Liverpool | Chiltern | XHCE | Chiltern Railways | |
| 68013 | Peter Wreford-Bush | 2691 | 29 August 2014 Liverpool | Chiltern | XHCE | Chiltern Railways | |
| 68014 | | 2692 | 29 August 2014 Liverpool | Chiltern | XHCE | Chiltern Railways | |
| 68015 | Kev Helmer | 2693 | 23 September 2014 Southampton | Chiltern | XHCE | Chiltern Railways | |
| 68016 | Fearless | 2694 | 24 October 2015 Workington | DRS | XHVE | DRS | |
| 68017 | Hornet | 2695 | 24 October 2015 Workington | DRS | XHVE | DRS | |
| 68018 | Vigilant | 2696 | 15 November 2015 Workington | DRS | XHVE | DRS | |
| 68019 | Brutus | 2697 | 15 November 2015 Workington | TPE | XHTP | TransPennine Express | |